Sex Savvy

A Lovemaking Guide
for Christian Wives

J. Parker

HHH Books

Sex Savvy
© 2013 by J. Parker

Published by HHH Books
Illustrations by Matt Baxter
Cover design by Melinda VanLone at Book Cover Corner

ISBN-13: 978-0615918471 (HHH Books)
ISBN-10: 0615918476

To my beloved husband.
We belong together.

"My beloved is mine and I am his."
Song of Songs 2:16a

Table of Contents

Preface

"You should write a book."

Since I began blogging at Hot, Holy & Humorous, I've heard *that* from someone or another. I pooh-poohed such suggestions. As far as I could tell, there were plenty of fabulous Christian books about sexuality from authors with better credentials than mine. Physicians, nurses, professors, theologians, ministers, professional speakers, and others have offered excellent treatment of God's biblical plan for physical intimacy.

My approach was focused instead on the kind of information and encouragement you should get from a best friend over a cup of coffee—you know, a gal-pal who offers helpful advice and the low-down on the low-down. Plus, it was all free. Free to anyone who wanted to read my blog.

But I had an epiphany while searching for an old post I'd written. I had difficulty finding the information I wanted, and *hello!* I *write* the blog. I realized that organizing posts into a book might be helpful. Moreover, when I looked at my site statistics, I noted that my how-to posts were particularly well-received.

Most Christian books on sexuality address anatomy, theology, attitude, and answers for specific problems. While these are all helpful, and I address them as well, many wives are still looking for specifics on *how*—how to have an orgasm, how to try new sexual positions, how to get in the mood, etc. There are secular resources for this approach, but not much from Christian authors.

So in response to my epiphany, I compiled *Sex Savvy: A Lovemaking Guide for Christian Wives*. You can read this book from front to back or by simply picking out the chapters that interest you. The material is primarily from my blog, but I've edited and added fresh illustrations. I pray that *Sex Savvy* helps Christian wives by giving biblical and blunt tips on how to have a better sex life that goes the distance and honors our Heavenly Father.

- *J*

Chapter 1
Kissing

Ah, the kiss! That brilliant invention of our Creator that makes us check our breath, cock our heads, plant a big wet one, and hunger for more. Plenty of Christians writing about sex believe that the orgasm is proof that our Creator designed mating for pleasure. While I agree, the kiss is an excellent example as well. After all, kisses are not required for reproduction, so what's their point?

Puh-leasure, people!

So pucker up and let's talk about kissing.

"Let him kiss me with the kisses of his mouth!"
Song of Songs 1:2

Types of Kisses

Kisses have been lauded for a long time as a beautiful expression of love between a man and a woman. Yet sometimes, we forget to keep the romance alive through tender and passionate kissing in our marriages.

In 1955, French actress Jeanne Bourgeois said: "A kiss can be a comma, a question mark, or an exclamation point." How true! The type of kiss can say a lot about what is going on between the two of you, and—like grammar—there is room for all kinds of punctuation.

Now there are types of kisses—from the quick peck to the soft exploring kiss to the open-mouthed twisting of tongues. They all have their place.

Butterfly kiss. This kiss is often given from parent to child and vice-versa. It involves blinking one's eyes to rub eyelashes against another's cheek or some other area of skin. It's sweet, but not particularly romantic. If you get hot and bothered from a butterfly kiss from your husband, it's been way too long since you had some nookie.

Peck. Pecks are those quick puckered-up kisses usually given in a hurry as one of you rushes out the door. A peck can also be a nice way of kissing in public without making everyone cover their eyes or puke. Pecks are great for what they are—a quick reminder that you love this person and cherish him.

Face kiss. This is simply one of you kissing the other anywhere on the face—cheek, forehead, nose, etc. A face kiss allows one of you to express affection or distract your spouse from whatever he/she is doing. Like if I'm writing here, and my husband starts kissing my forehead, cheek, chin...*Where was I?* Anyway, you get the idea. Soft kisses on the face are initiated by one partner, but usually appreciated by the other.

Soft lip kiss. My favorite! A soft lip kiss is leaning in and tenderly kissing one another's lips. Lips are parted like a cracked door or a hot dog bun—a small opening, but not too much. This soft kiss should last several seconds, to allow lingering on one another's delicious lips. It can be enjoyed by itself or as a teaser for a more passionate kiss. Many classic Hollywood kisses are soft lip kisses and leave us wanting more.

French kiss. I don't know why the French get credit for this one. Were they the only ones with tongues? I think not. It's also called "tongue hockey" (lovely, eh?). Basically, you tangle tongues and share saliva. A great French kiss is incredibly passionate and can tickle you all the way to your toes. A terrible French kiss chokes you or leaves you calling the HazMat team to clean up all the extra spit. Just remember to be gentle and flexible. Don't attack your husband's mouth; tease, explore, and enjoy it.

Licking kiss. A licking kiss involves your tongue stroking his tongue, teeth, lips, etc. This can be a titillating move, as long as you remember this is your honey's mouth and not the Tootsie Roll lollipop that you must reach the center of. Take it slow, and use your tongue lightly.

Nibbling kiss. How much should you involve your teeth in the process of kissing? Some people like to nibble on their spouse's lips. Notice I said "nibble," not "bite." Yes, vampires are all the rage, but if you feel a fangs-in impulse with your beloved…not cool. Keep it a nice soft use of your teeth. Of course, some people don't like this at all, so gauge your husband's pleasure as you try it.

I've described kissing types in reference to the lips, but you can pucker up, lick, and nibble almost anywhere on your husband's body (as long as he enjoys it too).

Here are a few questions to ask him:

What is your favorite type of kiss?

How important is kissing to you feeling loved and cherished?

How can I be a better kisser?

Do you want to kiss now?

Hopefully, that's the last question you'll get in before your lips and tongues entangle. It might lead to other things, or if your house is like mine, it might lead to your kids walking in and saying, "Eeewww!" Either way, it's a better use of a few seconds than whatever else you were going to do.

Tips for Kissing

Before you ever jumped into bed with your honey, I bet you tasted his lips, and there was something there that made you want to come back. Once we get married, however, some of that luscious lip-locking falls by the wayside, and we need a refresher course.

So here are a few tips for fantastic, fun-filled, fabulous, frisky, frenzied kissing.

Your breath. It matters. By the way, you are the last person to know whether you are experiencing a bout of halitosis. It's funny how we breathe onto our palms, sniff them, and expect that to tell us something. Do you smell your own sweat when you've been excessively exercising? Do your kids recognize when they have foot odor? No. Your breath will just smell like your breath to you, unless you make it smell minty or yummy. Toothpaste, mints, mouthwash—these are our friends. Use them. Especially if you just ate something with an intense taste or aroma.

Lips. Loose lips sink ships and communicate, "I can't be bothered to pucker." Tight lips indicate a controlling personality or anxiety. Relax your lips, but shape them so that they can be easily kissed.

Tongue. My worst kisser—a former date from long ago—had a twelve-foot tongue. Okay, maybe not. But he used it like a boa constrictor invading my mouth. If you're not sure how to use your tongue in an open-mouthed kiss, think of the word "tease." *Tease* your husband with your tongue. When full passion arrives, you can twist your tongues together to your heart's delight, but your tongue still shouldn't fill his entire mouth.

Hands. Where you place your hands is important. Kissing without touching can feel impersonal, yet immediately grabbing bums or private parts when going in for the smooch is not romantic. As your lips caress his lips, your hands should caress as well. You can caress shoulders, arms, back, hair, and face. You can also use your hands to draw your partner in or gently position him at a better angle.

Eyes. Open or closed? I'm not a stickler on this one. But some people think it's weird to be watched at such a close distance while being kissed, so they prefer closed. For some, blocking out visual stimuli also helps to concentrate on the sensation of the kiss.

You can enjoy kissing for its own beauty, or it can lead to something else. I wish I could do a quick survey and ask wives if they feel their husbands kiss them often enough without expecting further sexual activity. My prediction would be that many wives would say no.

If you doubt the wonderful gift of kissing from God, try it out for a while in your marriage. Jim Burns of the *Homeword* radio show suggests that married couples have a 15-second kiss every day. That might have a glorious effect on many couples—just returning to the courtship of kissing.

When His Kiss Tastes Bad

What if your husband's kiss tastes bad? One of my blog readers asked for tips on dealing with her husband who chewed tobacco. She loved to kiss, but his habit was a big turn-off.

Before I married, I dated one guy who dipped and one guy who smoked. While they didn't do it right before we kissed, such habits don't exactly scream, "Put your mouth on mine!" In fact, I've wondered where we even came up with such ideas. Who was the first person to stick a bunch of leaves in a piece of paper, roll it up, and light it inches from his mouth? Who first grabbed a wad of tobacco leaves and shoved it between his lip and teeth to gnaw on for a while?

Other substances in one's mouth can also make for a less-than-approachable set of lips—foods with pungent flavors, alcohol, or anything else you don't like. While you might wish that your honey would stop using whatever is turning you off, don't hold your breath. Especially when it comes to tobacco, it's hard to quit. It can be done, and I hope that your husband would make healthy choices for himself and for you, but it's a struggle and he may not quit. Yet, you still want to be able to smooch with your mate.

There seem to be two issues—what's actually going on with his mouth and how you think about it. Thus, you have a few options.

Talk to him. Tell your hubby that you love to kiss him and want to do so freely, but you are bothered by his habit. Ask that he brush his teeth, use a mouthwash, chew a fresh-breath gum, or suck on a mint before you two kiss. You might even come up with a cute way to remind him in the moment. Let's say he leans in for a smackeroo, and you ask, "Are you lickable?" or "Minty mouth or tobacco tongue?" Check in advance what kind of freshen-up-to-kiss reminders he'd prefer.

Vary your kisses. If you think he's been chewing or smoking or whatever, keep your kisses closed-mouth or kiss other places on him. Then as soon as you know his mouth is fresh, move in for the make-out. Don't be stingy with the kisses, but give clues as to when you are more interested in open-mouth kissing. He might notice the pattern and ask what's going on, or you can even explain. Hopefully, he'll understand that you do desire to put your mouth on his, but you feel more comfortable doing so when his mouth is clean.

Use a demonstration. This one depends on your husband's sense of humor. Read him carefully and proceed cautiously. But you might pick a substance that he hates and eat it in front of him. Then move in for a kiss and watch his reaction. If he flinches, then you can laugh and say something like, "What? You don't want a garlic kiss?" If you two laugh about it, you can explain that you feel the same way about the befouling substance he uses. (I could easily make this point in my house by devouring tuna fish and going in for the kill. My hubby, meanwhile, knows better than to kiss me after eating peanut butter; I jump away from his lips like a wild hokey-pokey move and wait for the fresh mouth.) Hopefully, your husband will understand your point and approach kissing accordingly.

Get over it. All that said, it won't hurt you to kiss someone who has been chewing, smoking, drinking, eating onions, etc. You can retrain your mind to focus on the physical sensations of the kiss. It will take time to move your thoughts away from "gross" to "great." But our brains are pretty powerful, and we can master our thought processes by practicing. If you want to try, simply use this approach when you begin to kiss: Every time your mind turns to the yuck factor, refocus to think about how his tongue is touching yours, or the feel of his hand on your back, or the texture of his hair as you run your hand through it. Get the idea? Over time, your mind will readjust, and you'll be able to think about the kiss more than the taste-bud-killer that was there an hour ago.

And when your dear hubby does present himself all fresh and kissable, make it worth his while.

Chapter 2
Cultivating Romance

Odds are that at some point in your relationship, your husband was romantic. Maybe it didn't come naturally and maybe it was only at the beginning, but something he did made you swoon a little.

Keeping romance alive has been the subject of plenty of self-help books, blogs, magazine articles, movies, and more. I'm not the truest romantic myself (for instance, I prefer most action films to chick flicks), but I agree that romance is an important aspect of marriage. So how do you keep that spark alive? Let's delve into non-romantic husbands and love letters.

**"If you find my love,
tell him that I am lovesick."
Song of Songs 5:8b (HCSB)**

When He's Not Romantic

I am married to Spock. Have you heard of him? My husband actually has a different name, but the personality is pretty much the same. Spock is the Vulcan character from the original *Star Trek* series (and recent movie reboot of the story). The defining characteristic of the Vulcan species is their ability to suppress emotion and focus entirely on what is logical.

Yep, that's my husband: *logical*.

Bringing your wife flowers for no reason is not logical. Buying expensive jewelry because it's pretty is not logical. Telling her that she's beautiful today when you already said it last week is not logical.

I'm not the only one married to someone who doesn't "get it" when it comes to beauty, spontaneity, and going the extra mile for a big gesture of love. So how do you get a guy like this to engage in romance in your marriage?

Here's what I've learned from my marriage to a Vulcan:

Take the lead. It does not occur to my husband to create a romantic environment for date night or lovemaking. Since I am the one who craves romance more — although he enjoys it — I take it upon myself to set the scene. I light the candles, I turn on the music,

I pour the bubble bath, or whatever. Putting forth a little effort can create an atmosphere where the only instruction left is "Simply Add ~~Water~~ Hubby."

Ask for romance. I need to hear that I am beautiful, that my husband desires me, that he loves me. Sometimes he forgets that. I used to be hurt by the omission. But after several years of marriage, I realized that my husband doesn't gush about his mother either, and she is downright heroic to him. Rather than feeling injured by his inattention, I invite his attention. For instance, I can put on my sexy nightie (or nudie) and ask, "So what do you think?" Or say, "You know what I like about your body?" and go through a list, followed by "What do you like about mine?" I have now opened the floor for him to express what I need to hear.

Establish routines. I had a friend whose husband's lack of affection hurt her feelings. She finally told him, "I need you to kiss me before you leave for work and kiss me when you get home." It became their routine. Was it forced at first? Yeah, a little. But now it's something they both enjoy—a romantic tradition.

Routines can be great for both of you. Demanding lots of spontaneous romance from a non-romantic guy is like mounting a Mount Everest expedition with a few Kit-Kat bars in your pack; don't get your hopes up. Asking your honey to introduce a romantic routine into

your relationship, though, is predictable and tangible—
something he can put on a to-do list and check off.
Perhaps the routine is a kiss or a hug at a certain time.
Perhaps he plans a date or a vacation for the two of you
on a special day each year (giving him plenty of time to
prepare). Perhaps the routine is that he undresses you
in particular way, noting as he goes all the beautiful
parts of your body. Just make the romantic tradition
something achievable for him and enjoyable to you.

Remember your hubby loves you. When your best
friend tells you how her romantic hubby swept her off
her feet with a surprise trip to a mountain cabin where
he cooked her favorite meal, serenaded her with his
guitar, and sprinkled the bed with rose petals before
making love to her, you may wonder why your
husband doesn't love you like that.

While I encourage husbands to up their game when
it comes to the romance department, some guys are
amazing at it and some guys aren't. Whether he has
natural wooing talent is not related to how much he
loves you.

Plenty of non-romantic guys would respond to "Do
you love your wife?" with an unequivocal "Of course."
In fact, it isn't logical to Mr. Spock to restate the
obvious over and over. So ask your husband to *tell* you
and to *show* you, and when he follows through,
remember that he is outside his comfort zone in

expressing the love for you that is well within his comfort zone. He loves you like crazy; he just needs cues to know how to demonstrate that love.

Enjoy the surprises. Since my guy isn't a hard-core romantic, I revel in those times when he goes above and beyond. For a recent birthday, my husband wrote me a love poem. A love poem! If you knew this guy— which you do if you ever watched the original *Star Trek*—you'd know how big a deal that is. I was on Cloud 9½ for the next month.

We wives should all enjoy the romance our husbands bring to marriage, but when it's not your guy's thing, those moments are super-sweet. Instead of thinking, "I wish he would do this more often," just enjoy the moment. Bask in it. Know how hard it was for him to make that effort, and how much that means he loves you.

Wives, do what you can to introduce the romance you want into your marriage. Your husband likely won't be as romantic as the hunk in the latest chick flick romance. He doesn't have a screenwriting team to come up with all of that for him. He's on his own. So help him out.

I can honestly say from my life with Spock that melding minds is far outweighed by melding hearts when we make the extra effort. (Plus, aren't those pointy ears kind of cute?)

How to Write a Love Letter

I've been asked about the best gift my husband ever got me, and hands-down it's the love poem he wrote. Now my husband is not the romantic type. I've fondly called him Spock on my blog because that's not far from his personality. Can you imagine a love letter written by a Vulcan?

My hubby's love letter to me would have likely made Cyrano de Bergerac cringe and yank the pen out of his hand, but it was absolutely beautiful to me because it required effort and thought as he expressed how much I mean to him.

Since we are not all naturally romantic like Robert and Elizabeth Barrett Browning (who traded love poems with verses like, "How do I love thee? Let me count the ways!"), I thought I'd give some tips for writing a love letter. Here are some components you might want to include:

Remember when. Recall a special memory you two shared. You could talk about when you first met or when you first knew that your husband was The One and how that time made you feel. Provide enough descriptive detail to recreate the scene and the emotions it evoked. Your memory could be romantic, funny, or a tale of triumph over hardship, as long as it's something that makes you both remember your courtship or marriage in a positive way.

SAMPLES

"I look back to the early days of our acquaintance; and Friendship, as to the days of Love and Innocence; and with an indescribable pleasure I have seen near a score of years roll over our Heads, with an affection heightened and improved by time—nor have the dreary years of absence in the smallest degree effaced from my mind the Image of the dear untitled man to whom I gave my Heart…"

—Abigail Adams to her husband, U.S. President John Adams

"All night long on my bed
I looked for the one my heart loves;
I looked for him but did not find him.
I will get up now and go about the city,
through its streets and squares;
I will search for the one my heart loves.
So I looked for him but did not find him.
The watchmen found me
as they made their rounds in the city.
'Have you seen the one my heart loves?'
Scarcely had I passed them
when I found the one my heart loves.
I held him and would not let him go…"

—Song of Songs 3:1-4

The best is yet to come. Write about your
anticipation of the future with your beloved. What do
you look forward to sharing with him? Is there
something specific you've talked about in your future?
Traveling? Settling down somewhere special? Making
love in the living room after the kids grow up and
move out? Whatever it is, let your husband know that
you expect to be with him for a long time and are
devoted to making your life together a good one.

SAMPLES

*"I will cover you with love when next I see you, with
caresses, with ecstasy. I want to gorge you with all the joys of
the flesh, so that you faint and die. I want you to be amazed
by me, and to confess to yourself that you had never dreamed
of such transports…When you are old, I want you to recall
those few hours, I want your dry bones to quiver with joy
when you think of them."*

—Gustave Flaubert (author) to his wife, Louise Colet
*"Let us hope and believe that we shall walk hand in hand
down the lengthening highway of life, one in heart, one in
impulse, and one in love, bearing each other's burdens,
sharing each other's joys, soothing each other's griefs. What
we will lose of youth, we will make up in love, so that the
account is squared, and to nobody's disadvantage. I love you,
my darling, and this my love will increase, step by step as
tooth by tooth falls out, mile-stoning my way down to the
great mystery and the Sweet Bye & Bye."*

—Mark Twain (Samuel Clemens) to his wife, Olivia Langdon

What turns you on. We all want to feel attractive to our mate, so describe what features of his appearance are appealing to you. What about his looks turns you on? Avoid the basic, "You're handsome or "You're hot" statements, and get specific. Name parts of the body (eyes, mouth, legs, toenails, whatever) and tell what you like about them.

SAMPLES

"How beautiful you are, my darling!

> *Oh, how beautiful!*

> *Your eyes behind your veil are doves.*

Your hair is like a flock of goats

> *descending from Mount Gilead.*

Your teeth are like a flock of sheep just shorn,

> *coming up from the washing.*

Each has its twin;

> *not one of them is alone.*

Your lips are like a scarlet ribbon;

> *your mouth is lovely.*

Your temples behind your veil

> *are like the halves of a pomegranate.*

Your neck is like the tower of David,

> *built with elegance;*

on it hang a thousand shields,

> *all of them shields of warriors.*

Your two breasts are like two fawns,
like twin fawns of a gazelle
that browse among the lilies."
—Song of Songs 4:1-5
"My lover is radiant and ruddy,
outstanding among ten thousand.
His head is purest gold;
his hair is wavy
and black as a raven.
His eyes are like doves
by the water streams,
washed in milk,
mounted like jewels.
His cheeks are like beds of spice
yielding perfume.
His lips are like lilies
dripping with myrrh.
His arms are rods of gold
set with chrysolite.
His body is like polished ivory
decorated with sapphires."
—Song of Songs 5:10-14

The beauty within. No one wants to feel like they are only appreciated for their appearance. Sure, we want to be beautiful—but we also want our beauty to go deeper. God has given your man some special qualities that you appreciate, so name them. Is your honey humorous? Trustworthy? Smart? Handy? Generous? A good father? Consider pointing out specific character traits as reasons you love him and write them down.

SAMPLES

"I love your verses with all my heart, dear Miss Barrett, — and this is no off-hand complimentary letter that I shall write—whatever else, no prompt matter-of-course recognition of your genius and there a graceful and natural end of the thing: since the day last week when I first read your poems, I quite laugh to remember how I have been turning and turning again in my mind what I should be able to tell you of their effect upon me…"

—Robert Browning (poet) in his first letter to his wife, Elizabeth Barrett Browning (also poet)

"I already love in you your beauty, but I am only beginning to love in you that which is eternal and ever precious—your heart, your soul."

—Count Leo Tolstoy (author) to his fiancée, Valeria Arsenev

Thank God for your mate. Give thanksgiving to the Creator for the gift of your husband. In Philippians 1:3, the Apostle Paul says: "I thank my God every time I remember you." Wouldn't it be nice to know that your husband does the same? Let your beloved know that he is one of the best blessings God ever gave you.

SAMPLES

"How full of joy & happiness the world seemed to me, for I felt that you are my own Nell—that you love me! I said, 'I am content.' I was happy and thanked God that he had so blessed me!"

—U.S. President Chester Arthur to his wife, Ellen Lewis Herndon

"Each morning, as I rise
I give thanks to God
For your presence
lying next to my bod"

—"Spock" to J on her birthday

Describe your love. Here are some final tips for describing your love.

Use nicknames if you have them. Winston Churchill (British prime minister) and his wife Clementine called each other "Pug" and "Cat" in their letters, and the couple in Song of Songs called each other "Beloved."

Include analogies if you have any. Try it out in your head first by completing statements like "Being with you is like _____" and "You are to me like ____ is to ____."

Stay away from clichés. "Roses are red, violets are blue" ain't gonna cut it, unless your next two lines are utterly brilliant. Also, his eyes may indeed "sparkle like the stars," but try to come up with something fresh.

Gush a little. Yes, it's okay to write stuff that would make your teenager want to vomit if he/she read it.

Keep it going. One love letter is awesome. *Continuing* this practice can be a great way to remind yourself why you love your husband and to be reminded why he loves you. The Brownings wrote 574 love letters to one another, and Winston and Clementine Churchill wrote throughout their 57-year marriage. We need to hear now and then not only that we are loved, but also why we are loved. Love letters are a great way to express that sentiment to your spouse.

Chapter 3
Finding Time

"We've got 15 minutes!"

I fear this statement, or something like it, is said rather often in marriages. But far worse are those who seem to have zero minutes for sexual intimacy. How can couples find time to connect physically when the rest of life demands so much of our time?

"All night long on my bed I looked for the one my heart loves;
I looked for him but did not find him."
Song of Songs 3:1

Scheduling Sex

My best friend and I have a routine. We text back and forth about our calendars, find an open date, and schedule time to meet up for breakfast or lunch. Once a week or so, you could find us at a restaurant table for a social/work day. There are some predictable parts: We will eat. We will chat. We will work on our respective laptops. But there's no agenda, no script. Sometimes we meet for an hour or two; other times we hunker down for maybe six hours of productivity. Sometimes we have serious discussions; sometimes we laugh ourselves so silly I wonder if others might be saying to the wait staff, "I'll have what they're having." Sometimes I'm good and get a salad; sometimes I get the juicy burger. *Always*, I enjoy our time together.

Why don't we treat sex in marriage this way? Of all the controversial topics about marital sexuality, scheduling sex continues to invite argument, with both advocates and naysayers. For all those who swear that scheduling sex has increased their marital intimacy, there are plenty who reject the notion that scheduling sex is a good idea for their marriage. The naysayers are certain that putting sex on a schedule results in contrived, obligatory sex rather than passionate lovemaking.

But like lunch dates with my friend, there's no agenda, no script. Scheduling sex with your husband is merely prioritizing that activity enough to put it on your respective calendars. This can be especially important with spouses whose schedules rarely align or who juggle children's activities.

Once you get there—to your scheduled sex appointment—you can order whatever you want. You might have a quickie or hours-long lovemaking. You might stay in the bedroom or change up your location. You might go for the tried-and-true or spice it up with a new sexual activity or position. Spontaneity still exists in *what* you do together.

Try scheduling sex a few times, and see how it goes. It might feel forced at first, but so does that first lunch date with a friend. Once you get in a groove, you might find yourself happy with the results.

How to start. Many couples schedule once a week. They may get in other lovemaking sessions over those seven days, but most couples should be making love at least once a week. Ask your husband: "When are you free this week to have some *us time*?" Give a wink while saying "us time" and he might get the hint. Or you could come right out and say, "I want to carve out time for us to have sex this week. What day/evening is good for you?" But try not to make it like scheduling an office conference. Instead, view it like setting up a lunch date or a night out with a friend. Create anticipation of the experience as you describe your eagerness for time together.

How to show up. All that's required when scheduling sex is that you show up and be willing to have sex at the time you committed to. If you have further expectations or desires for that time, express them when you arrive. Otherwise, fall into each other's arms and see what happens. There's no agenda unless you make one. If you're among those who really desire spontaneity and struggle with this concept of scheduling, set the scene a little with music, candles, or whatever to help you get in the mood. Take deep breaths and remind yourself that this time is like any other hour in your day and you can make of it what you want.

How to evaluate. Don't make up your mind based on the first time. The first time you do anything can be awkward, but it might be exactly what you come to love within a short time. Show up a second and a third time and see if you two get in a groove—a Barry White kind of groove. Get a few times under your belt and then see how you both feel about it.

How to make it fun. Here are some ways couples have suggested for making scheduling sex more fun:

Buy a wall or desk calendar and mark those days with hearts or lips or some other sexy reminder. You could even introduce your own code. Write "YAM" for "you and me" time, or "RMW" for "rock my world." Be creative.

Build anticipation by flirting about the upcoming appointment. Plant a big kiss on your honey in the morning before you go to work and say, "Plenty more of that coming tonight." Or text your husband, "Guess what I'm *not* wearing. You can see for yourself tonight. ;)" Find other ways to reference how you are looking forward to your special time.

Take turns planning other aspects of the event. You could put the date on the calendar, and one time hubby chooses the place and you choose the position, and then vice versa. Or each of you has an opportunity to create the scene before the other arrives.

Make it a secret habit. If you both know that every Sunday afternoon after church, you and your husband will be climbing the peak of pleasure, it can become your playful little secret.

Those nights of scheduled sex might become a happy tradition in your marriage. Give it a shot!

Unmatched Bedtimes

Some of you are married to night owls who come alive at the stroke of midnight, while others have husbands with that annoying habit of waking up early, throwing open the curtains, and greeting the morning whistling songs at the highest decibels possible. (Can you tell which I am?) And very often, a night owl marries a morning person. As if you didn't have enough to work through with the family backgrounds and gender differences!

I chalk it up to another humorous part of marital sexuality—trying to get those schedules matched so that we can both enjoy some face-to-face, body-to-body time. Sometimes what gets in the way of getting it on is simply that you are exhausted by 11:00 p.m. and he's raring to go. Or you're up at the crack of dawn and have plenty of early-morning energy to make love while he's sprawled across the bed snoring and drooling into the pillow. What to do? What to do?

Perhaps you should benefit from my years of experience on what *doesn't* work: Straddling his sleeping body and bouncing may arouse his little guy, but the big guy is still pretty dang tired and not so happy that he's awake. Demanding in a hostile tone that he stay up later or wake up earlier is not likely to lead to a morning/evening of memorable lovemaking. Trying to get the kids to bed earlier so you can enjoy time before one of you dozes off midsentence will work for one or two nights; then, the little knee-biters will consult their union manual and stage a rather effective protest.

What does work? Negotiation. Compromise. (Don't we married people *love* those words?)

Keeping similar bedtimes fosters opportunity for sexual intimacy in your marriage. It's a great idea. Waking up together also encourages time together—for physical and emotional connection.

Maybe your compromise is that the night owl goes to bed to earlier and then gets back up after his/her spouse falls asleep. Maybe you negotiate days of the week to go to bed early and days to sleep in. Maybe one of you simply shifts the schedule to match the other for now, knowing that it can change in the future. (For instance, a stay-at-home mom might shift to her husband's early schedule if she can manage a nap sometime in the day.) It's worth discussing your mismatched schedules to find a solution so that you can spend more time together.

Too many couples have one spouse crawling into bed early, while the other stays up watching television late into the night. In the morning, the early-to-bed one is indeed early-to-rise, and the night owl wakes long after. And before you know it, two people who vowed to love and cherish, be there for one another, and grow in intimacy daily pass each other like ships in the night. You lose your sense of emotional closeness, and the physical closeness fades as well. That's not the way it's meant to be.

Make it a priority to be *in bed with your husband* at times when you are both awake—morning or night. It will give you a chance to talk and spend time together. And that will cultivate those moments of "Hey, while we're here..." Then enjoy!

Drive-thru Sex: The Quickie

What is a *quickie*? According to Dictionary.com, it's simply "a hurried sexual encounter." A quickie can be any sexual encounter—intercourse, oral sex, hand job, etc.—that occurs in a brief span of time. Personally, I would break down sexual encounters as follows:

Extended lovemaking = 5-star restaurant. Most of us don't go out to posh restaurants all of the time. Those five-course meals that pamper our palate are a treat we enjoy on special occasions.

Usual sex = Family restaurant. This is the place in our neighborhood where we know the menu, have a few favorites, and enjoy an hour or so of good dining. Nothing fancy, but definitely satisfying.

Quickie = Drive-thru. Pick a fast food place, get it on the go, and eat fast. Not recommended as a standard for meals but sates the hunger and can be yummy.

Just like passing through your McDonald's or Taco Bell drive-thru, there are some things to remember when approaching the quickie.

Make up your mind quickly. This ain't a white-tablecloth restaurant where the suited server will wait for as long as you wish to peruse the menu before ordering. You drive up, glance at the menu choices, and lean over to the speaker to order. If you try taking

12 minutes to figure out what you want, you may end up with a traffic jam of angry drivers behind you honking their horns and yelling.

Likewise, if you and your husband want to have a quickie, decide fast what you mean. Are you performing a hand job for him? Will you have intercourse? Is orgasm a must for you? Keep the expectations clear for what you're doing so you can enjoy it for what it is. If you try taking 12 minutes to figure out what you want, you may end up with a traffic jam of needy children knocking at your door and yelling.

Speak up clearly. Those drive-thru speakers are not exactly high tech. If you want your order to arrive with some semblance of what you want, you'd better speak loudly and enunciate. You don't want the attendant hearing "pies" when you said "fries."

With the quickie, you must also speak up clearly. This is no time to be patient while hubby slowly strokes the area around where you want to be touched until 10 minutes later he finds the spot. Speak up! Move his hand and say things like, "Right here feels good" or "That's the spot." Tell him if something hurts, feels good, or would be better another way. Speak up so he can get the order right.

Be prepared for grease. Despite the inclusion of salads on many fast-food menus, let's face it: Most drive-thru food is greasy. The foods are fried in oil, slathered in butter, or have a naturally high content of fat. You know that going in, so you aren't surprised when you bite into that battered chicken strip and juices seep out.

Bring out the grease with the quickie too! In other words, lubrication is key. Have your personal lubricant or coconut oil ready to go. If you're doing a hand job — which I've sometimes called a "lube job" — you'll probably need to add moisture. For intercourse, most wives take a substantial amount of time to become "wet" enough for penetration. You likely won't have time with a quickie, so get out the lubricant and start with it.

Eat quickly. Um, yeah. Not going to describe this one. Use your imagination.

Leave satisfied. Admittedly it's not the dining experience I'm going to write a magazine review about, but I like some drive-thru food. It addresses my hunger. It fills my tummy. It hits the spot.

Similarly, the quickie should not be the go-to sexual encounter in marriage, but it has its place. There are times when longer intimate experiences are not possible. You're at the in-laws', your children are young and need regular supervision, your work schedules don't match up, or whatever. You wouldn't go without food simply because you don't have time to make it a three-course meal. Likewise, your marriage need not go without sex because time is currently in short supply. The quickie can sate your hunger and hit the spot.

One more tip: **Build anticipation before you drive through.** It will be much easier to enjoy that quickie if you and hubby are flirting and doing small things for one another throughout the day. You won't have much time for foreplay with the quickie, so your foreplay is all of those things you do with and for each other outside of the bedroom. If you invest in your friendship, affection, and desire for one another, it can be a smoother transition to your hubby looking at you and saying, "Quick, let's have sex!" The quickie will become a brief physical expression of the longer experiences of deep love you've had outside the bedroom.

Chapter 4
Getting Ready for Sex

*Have you noticed that women in movies always seem
ready for sex? As if that's been on their mind all day long? In
reality, most wives spend their day navigating mundane
tasks, like performing their day job, determining what to cook
for dinner, managing all that laundry.*

*Alas, sometimes you have to prepare your mind and body
for sexual intimacy with your husband. So let's talk about
lingerie and then getting yourself ready for that intimate
encounter with your man.*

"Take me away with you—let us hurry!"
Song of Songs 1:3

How to Shop for Lingerie

Lingerie can include anything from a camisole and briefs to a long nightgown to a leather teddy. Whatever your idea of pretty, you can probably find something to wear to bed…and to let hubby remove. Lingerie can make you feel sexy and show you're making additional effort to appeal to your husband sexually.

Here are my tips for shopping for lingerie:

Fabrics. One of the standard complaints about alluring lingerie is that it's itchy or scratchy. Look for comfortable fabrics. Oftentimes, this means spending a little more, but not always. Cotton, silk, and satin will feel better than polyester, lace, and fake leather. If you want a lacy look, you may find a comfortable choice with the lace overlaid on a softer fabric.

But don't worry too much about checking labels or asking, "What's this made of?" Just touch the fabric. Stroke a small section in your hands and ask whether you want that fabric rubbing against your skin. Then buy what feels soft and sexy.

Body type. What looks and feels good on a tall, thin woman isn't the same as what looks and feels good on a petite, buxom woman. Lingerie should play to your assets, while minimizing those areas that thrill you less.

Full-figured? Consider a babydoll, teddy, or two-piece design that is fitted around the bust and flares out toward the hemline. This will emphasize the bust but camouflage any extra inches around the torso. Remember that dark colors are slimming, so stay away from whites and pastels.

Tall & thin? A standard bra or camisole-and-panties combination flatters this figure. If you're willing, a garter belt will emphasize long legs.

<u>Short & petite?</u> Try a chemise or gown with a slit up the leg. This will make your legs appear longer, drawing the eye up toward the torso.

<u>Athletic build?</u> Boy shorts and "cheekies" emphasize muscular legs and a nice derrière. Pair them with a bra, camisole, or even a corset.

<u>Bra/corset tips.</u> Smaller busts look good in triangle bras or balconette styles. Average busts look good in

demi (half-cup) and push-up styles. Larger busts look good with a full cup or plunge.

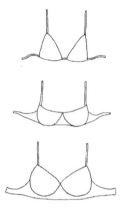

These guidelines aren't hard and fast, of course—just ideas to consider.

Your best bet is to enlist the help of a salesperson. They should be able to point out options for your shape and assets. Look through the store with an eye toward what will help you focus on your best attributes and feel confident.

Fit. Double-check your size. If you buy too small, you'll be uncomfortable, and the garment won't hang well. If you buy too big, it won't show off your assets.

If it's been a while, get a bra fitting from a reputable store. Also, try on different sizes of lingerie in the dressing room. Remember that bra and undies should provide full coverage to look their best.

Comfort. A wife wants to feel confident about her body when she puts on lingerie. For some ladies, that means a black-and-red corset and a thong. For others, that means a silky nightgown with matching robe.

When buying lingerie that both hubby and wife can enjoy, consider your comfort level. Buy something that stretches you a little, but not too much. If you're in a sleep shirt most nights, you probably wouldn't feel comfortable donning nipple tassels and crotchless panties (at least not right away). Find something like what you already wear, but a little edgier, sexier, and more revealing.

For both of you. This lingerie experience is not solely for him. Sometimes men can communicate that message unwittingly (or wittingly). Most wives want to be appreciated, desired, beautiful...but not ogled like a 16-oz prime rib at your local steakhouse. You aren't being served on a platter. You're presenting your body in beautiful attire to appeal to your husband and to feel confident about the beauty that God gave you. Look for lingerie that accomplishes that.

Prepping for Sex

You are planning or he is hoping to have sex soon. But right now, you're in that take-it-or-leave-it mood. Or maybe even a leave-it-or-leave-it mood. *sigh*

If you waited to be perfectly "in the mood" every single time to have sex, some of your marriages wouldn't experience another sexual encounter for months. Some of you would get lucky this weekend, but you are supposed to be having sex tonight.

Thankfully, it's not about being in the mood, as if you stand around and suddenly get hit by the lightning bolt of lovemaking. You can create some electricity yourself. You can get in the mood. So here are some tips on how to prepare yourself for sex. You can try one or more and see what works for you.

Build anticipation. We tend to enjoy what we anticipate. Got a vacation coming up? A birthday? A massage? We think ahead about what that will be like and plan how much we will enjoy its arrival. Try doing the same thing with sexual intimacy in your marriage. Think ahead about when you'll make love later.

If you're planning a night of hot-and-heavy, let images come to mind throughout the day. Think about the attractiveness of your husband, the way you felt the last time he kissed you or when you last climaxed, the joy of becoming physically one flesh, and the gift of sex from God. Pray that your evening will go well, and that you'll both find pleasure and connection with one another. Let the anticipation build, and your body may respond with more readiness when the moment arrives.

Remove distraction. One of the greatest difficulties for wives is distraction. Female brains are typically able to juggle more balls than a Las Vegas act. We have so much else going on in our lives and around our houses that asking us to focus on sex is like asking that juggler to toss a single ball. We get antsy.

But you won't be able to relax and enjoy the pleasure of sex with your husband unless you focus. Do your best to remove distractions. This can include getting the kids to bed early, straightening up the bedroom, putting away your to-do list—whatever you need to do to put down those balls and get into The Act.

Prepare location. Atmosphere matters. We instinctively know this when we enter restaurants and get an immediate feel for the food based on the surroundings. Likewise, we can create a mood by preparing the location of our lovemaking. That might mean taking the time to refurbish your bedroom to make it a pleasant place, adding ambiance enhancers like candlelight and music, or creating an inviting space for the two of you to feel as excited as a pair of mating-season rabbits. It could even be a simple as getting the Legos and the Barbies out of your bedroom.

Consider what environment would evoke your romantic and sexy side. Then make the effort to have your bedroom reflect that environment.

Awaken sensation. We have five senses—sight, smell, hearing, touch, and taste. Sexual intimacy is particularly focused on sight and touch but can involve all five senses. To get in the mood, try to awaken those senses. You can light a scented candle and inhale deeply; turn on a sexual intimacy playlist and close your eyes to listen; take a bubble bath and feel the hot water and foam stroke your skin; replace your regular sheets with satin ones; bring chocolate-covered strawberries or champagne into the bedroom.

Think of things that are not specifically sexual, but rather sensual. Find ways to awaken your senses, so that you'll be ready when your senses are engaged in lovemaking.

Ask for affection. Wives often need more affectionate foreplay before feeling ready to make love. Let's be honest, ladies: Holding off a horny husband from going straight to the erogenous zones can be like defending your kingdom with a Nerf sword. At some point, you want to yell, "Hey! Hold hands first, handle hooha later!"

Yet, one of the sexiest things *ever* is your husband stroking you gently with his broad, manly hands. Or that soft-lipped, melting-into-each-other kiss that lingers until the tingle runs all the way down to your pinkie toes. Ask for the affection you need. Explain that you might get in the mood if you could spend some time touching, kissing, snuggling, or getting a massage. Ten to fifteen minutes of that, and you might be eager to make love when you weren't before.

Use communication. Here are two things to remember: Most husbands love to turn us wives on, and most husbands cannot read their wives' minds.

So tell him what feels good. You can use words, moans, shrieks, whatever, but communicate clearly what you enjoy in the bedroom. It can feel awkward at first to say things like, "Over here is better" or "I love it when you ___," but the initial discomfort passes and most husbands are receptive to positively-phrased suggestions.

Pay attention. Whatever preparation you've done before, you still need to pay attention to what's happening in the moment. Once you come together with your husband, think about what's happening to your body and to his body. You can open your eyes and watch your bodies melding or gaze at his facial expressions. Or you can close your eyes and focus on the nerves of your skin as they awaken with his touch.

Hone in on your erogenous zones and focus your mental energy on their arousal.

If your mind wanders, simply bring it back to the moment at hand. You might need to do this a few times before your mind is fully engaged. But do your best to give that time of sexual intimacy your full, undivided attention.

Using these tips to prepare yourself for sex, you might find yourself more in the mood for lovemaking than you originally felt. Hopefully, you can get turned on as you progress into this sexual encounter with your husband.

Chapter 5
Having Oral Sex

There's a chapter in Kevin Leman's excellent book, Sheet Music, *about oral sex. I once loaned my copy to a good friend, and her husband looked through the table of contents and immediately flipped to that chapter. There is something very appealing about this practice to some people. So what's the hubbub all about?*

"My beloved has gone down to his garden, to the beds of spices,
to browse in the gardens and to gather lilies."
Song of Songs 6:2

Is Oral Sex Okay with God?

According to most modern biblical scholars, the Song of Songs is about the sexual love between a married couple. In this Old Testament book, preserved as part of the holy scriptures, specific sexual acts are described. There appear to be at least two references to oral sex within—the first woman to man, the second man to woman.

"Like an apple tree among the trees of the forest, so is my beloved among the young men. In his shade I took great delight and sat down, and his fruit was sweet to my taste" *(Song of Songs 2:3).*

"Awake, O north wind, and come, wind of the south; make my garden breathe out fragrance, let its spices be wafted abroad. May my beloved come into his garden and eat its choice fruits!" (Song of Solomon 4:16).

Moreover, there is nothing inherently harmful about oral sex. There isn't much research into the composition or possible health benefits, but a wife's natural lubricant appears to be okay for her husband to ingest. The contact of lips and tongue to genitals is not far different from hands or fingers on genitals. No stretching or painful penetration is part of the process.[1]

---

[1] Some have compared oral and anal sex. There is no comparison. The rectum contains harmful bacteria, is not designed for penetration, and

The one caveat is that sexually transmitted diseases and infections can be passed by oral-genital contact, so if that is an issue in your marriage, be aware.

With possible biblical precedent and no harmful physical effects, what are the objections to oral sex? Some believe it is unnatural to engage in sex that doesn't involve penetration. However, sexual encounters involve foreplay, which isn't penetration. This is simply touching of another sort.

Some believe it is wrong because it is portrayed in pornography. Well, so is penetration. While I strongly warn against viewing pornography and attempting to copy what is seen there, plenty of people who've never seen a porn film engage in fellatio and cunnilingus. They didn't get the idea from porn.

Also, Julie Sibert of *Intimacy in Marriage* has pointed out that kissing one another's bodies is quite all right. So where do the lips stop kissing? Must they stop before reaching genitalia? Inner thigh okay? Vulva not? Without biblical, health, or practical reasons, I don't see why that area is forbidden.

Of course, you must decide for yourself and live out your life in good conscience before God. Just don't allow preconceived notions to decide for you. Search it

---

usually involves pain for the woman.

out for yourself. Decide based on the merits whether oral sex will be on your marital intimacy menu.

For Him (Fellatio)

Here's a glimpse at my internal conversation while preparing for my first blog post on oral sex:

Me: I should do a post on giving blow jobs.

I: What are you going to say about blow jobs?

Me: You know, a how to.

I: You're going to describe how to give a blow job? Are you crazy!

Me: Some wives might want a little coaching.

I: Are you actually going to call it a "blow job"?

Me: That's what everyone calls it.

I: How about "fellatio"?

Me: If I call it fellatio, no one will know what I'm talking about.

I: How about "the thing that must not be named."

Me: Isn't that Voldemort from Harry Potter?

I: Your brain is too distracted.

Me: Not when I'm giving a blow job. I'm really focused then.

I: So that you don't choke?

Me: Well, yeah. And because it's kinda hot. You know, "his fruit is sweet to my taste," from Song of Songs?

I: So you're actually going to talk about this in public?

Me: Um, maybe.

I: Well, if you do, don't take me down with you.

Me: *"Take me down with you."* That's funny.

I: *rolls eyes*

Sources that describe how to give a "blow job" usually do not have a Christian perspective and may use photography or graphic images. Perhaps some have learned how to from watching a porn film. Meanwhile, I have never seen a porn film. (I put it in the ranks of heroin; I don't need to try it to know I don't need to try it.) But I have gained wisdom about this activity through the years, and oral sex is biblical if desired by both partners.

Some husbands would like their wives to "go down" on them, and some wives would be willing to give it a shot or want to try it again.[2] Some of those wives feel that they don't know what to do or how to do it. So here I go with a short how-to lesson on giving a blow job.

Do you really blow? No. Please do not treat your husband's opening like the end of a balloon and attempt to inflate it with your breath. A blow job is merely the slang term for a woman inserting a man's penis into her mouth. What happens after that determines whether it is a good blow job or a lame one.

How much of his penis do I put in my mouth? It can vary. You can put your mouth only around the

_____

[2] If your husband has a sexually-transmitted disease or you're worried he may have one, be aware that STDs can spread with oral-genital contact.

head of the penis, move your mouth over the shaft, or even deep-throat your husband's penis (explained below). This isn't about swallowing your husband. It's about providing oral stimulation to his sensitive genital area. While providing oral stimulation, you will need to breathe mostly through your nose.

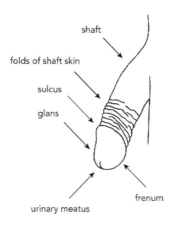

What do I do with my mouth? We've established that you don't blow, but you do kiss, lick, and suck with your lips and tongue. The tongue, in fact, can be very important in stimulation. These can be small licks around the ridge, head, and tip, or longer licks up and down the shaft of the penis to the head. With the penis inside your mouth, you can also pump your tongue a little to increase pressure. Sucking also increases the pressure, especially as you move your mouth up and down his penis. You can add your hand to the mix; that is, simultaneously use your hand(s) to provide slight pressure and a different feel as your mouth works. For the first time out, imagine the head of the penis as an ice cream cone and the shaft as a fudgsicle. That might help a little.

Where does it feel best for him? The greatest concentration of nerve endings is in the head of a man's penis. While stimulating the shaft also feels good, the ridge between the shaft and head, the head itself, and the tip are all more sensitive. Licking, sucking, and oral pressure in that area will likely feel particularly good. That said, you can't just hang out there doing the same thing over and over. The best sex involves variation, and that goes for oral sex as well.

What is "deep-throating"? To deep throat during a blow job means to put the penis so far into your mouth that the head makes contact with your throat. The throat is a tighter space and can provide more pressure and friction. Here's some advice if you want to give it a try: Open your throat, and widen your mouth to an aperture larger than your husband's penis so that you can continue to breathe around it. Also, don't expect to stay in that position for long. You can throat the tip and then move back out. The motion may feel better to your husband anyway.

Should I spit or swallow? Some women do not want semen in their mouth, period—either because they do not want to waste the sperm (a principle in Catholicism) or because they are simply repulsed by the thought of this liquid in their mouth. If you are one of them, you'll need to make sure that you pull your mouth away well in advance. If your husband reaches the "point of no return," he will begin ejaculation whether your mouth is there or not.

If you are willing to allow his ejaculate into your mouth, then you have to figure out what to do. First, you should know that swallowing semen is not in any way harmful to your body. Second, you might ask whether it would offend you if your husband gave you oral sex but made a big deal about disliking your lubrication. Third, if you don't want to swallow, be polite about spitting. Have a cup handy on the night table or somewhere nearby, hold the liquid in your mouth, and then spit it into the cup. You can also use a hand towel. You can always go to the bathroom to brush your teeth and/or use mouthwash to clear out the taste. For those willing to swallow, the consistency and taste of semen can vary; its consistency is like a beaten egg, but it tastes sweet to salty. If you're worried about your waistline, semen contains vitamins, sodium, and fructose and ranges between 5 to 25 calories—hardly a diet killer.

What if I give my husband a blow job, and I don't like it? Will I have to do it again? There is *no* rule that you must have oral sex as part of an intimate relationship. Plenty of sexually satisfied couples don't. That said, ask yourself what you didn't enjoy about the experience. Did you dislike certain sensations? Did your jaw hurt? (It might.) Is the problem something that could be adjusted the next time around? If you genuinely do not want to engage in this activity in the future, tell your husband. Try not to say something like, "That was so yuck!" He may take it personally that you don't want to make oral contact with his manhood. You can simply explain that you felt very uncomfortable and that you prefer other activities as part of your sex life. You might even suggest one. Perhaps you don't want to perform fellatio, but you're willing to do strip-tease for him or introduce an appropriate sex toy or give him a hand job.

How can my husband help to make this a positive experience? The first caveat is that you should be allowed to remain in control of your mouth. That is, if you need to pull away and take a break, then he should understand that. In a moment of extreme pleasure, a man might want to hold his wife's head and pull her mouth into him. This often isn't a good idea; men are stronger than they sometimes realize, and this action can make it difficult for the woman to control the motions in such a way that she remains comfortable throughout.

Another point is that husbands should communicate what feels good. He can talk you through it or make happy noises when you've hit a really great spot. You can even talk ahead of time so that he can show you on his penis where his most pleasurable places are. You can discuss how it felt afterward so that you know what worked best and what he might like next time.

Finally, he can affirm you. A constant for many women is that we like to be appreciated when we go out of our way to do something. Well, here's an opportunity for a husband to say nice things about his wife for her willingness to focus the sexual experience on his pleasure. Some wives also get a lot of pleasure from giving blow jobs.

"Like an apple tree among the trees of the forest
is my lover among the young men.
I delight to sit in his shade,
and his fruit is sweet to my taste."
—Song of Songs 2:3

For Her (Cunnilingus)

In the previous chapter, I treated you to the internal dialogue I had before writing about fellatio. How about another peek into my brain? (Be afraid. Be very afraid.)

Me: What should I call this post?

I: How about "Lie Back and Think of England?"

Me: No. "Lie back and think of England" is what that crazy Brit lady said to make women think sex isn't enjoyable. How about "Lie Back and Think of Tinglin'"? That's more like it!

I: Seriously?

Me: Sorta seriously. I could just call it "Goin' Down." Bow chicka wow-wow.

I: You are going down…into the gutter, girlfriend. What's wrong with you?

Me: Quite a few things. For one, I can't cook all that well. Plus, my nose is kind of big. And my—

I: No, no. I mean, why do you always joke about sex?

Me: Um…'cause it's funny?

I: You think sex is funny?

Me: Don't you? Hey, I'm about to tell a group of Christian wives why spreading their legs and letting hubbies' mouths touch their private parts can be kinda nice. I'm even going to mention how it's actually in the Bible! I sure didn't know that when I was a teen. If that had been mentioned in my *"becoming a woman"* Bible class, I would have fallen out of my chair from embarrassment or laughter or both.

I: *You're digressing. How about "Oral Sex: Better to Give and Receive"?*

Me: *I like it! Let's go.*

Believe it or not, a lot of hubbies would like to get their wives tinglin' down there. Several husbands have reported on my blog being physically aroused and emotionally moved by the openness of their wives when *she* is on the receiving end of oral sex.

Yet plenty of wives are nervous, resistant, or downright opposed to receiving cunnilingus (the scientific term for a woman receiving oral sex). For whatever reason, the idea of their husband's mouth on their privates does not sound appealing. As before—with fellatio—I'm going to give some basic information. Perhaps after learning more about it, you may open up to the experience—figuratively and literally.

What's so pleasurable about oral sex? First of all, the focus is the wife. While sex should be mutually satisfying, there are benefits to focusing on one spouse or the other from time to time. Husbands can get a big kick out of getting their wife's engine purring.

Second, it is a different and delicate sensation. I'm back to my frozen treat example. Have you ever held an ice cream cone and eaten it this way and that way? You can slurp with your tongue all the way across; give little licks along the edge or at the whipped top; suck the cream with your mouth; twirl your tongue around; brush your lips against the coolness; come at the ice cream straight on, sideways, or from any angle. Your mouth is a handy tool. Now imagine you, lovely wife, are the ice cream. Can you see why that might feel good?

Third, your husband likes that perspective. For one thing, your husband's eyes are close to his mouth, and he can see what he's doing, gauge your body's response, and revel in your pleasure. Let me cite some husbands' comments from my blog about the appeal of giving cunnilingus:

"She is totally open to me and I am giving her incredible pleasure."

"I've...always loved giving my wife oral (sexually, it is probably my favorite thing to do)."

"She is then totally open, giving herself totally over to me."

"I am a husband who loves going down on my wife. I really enjoy experiencing her orgasm from that perspective, it is truly amazing."

Fourth, it is one of the easier ways for a woman to orgasm. Because the husband can directly stimulate the clitoris, the mouth provides lubrication with saliva, and the mouth can vary in intensity, many wives report experiencing climax during oral sex.

What do you need to do to enjoy receiving oral sex?
Just "lie back and think of tinglin'? Sort of. Yes. Because
you need to relax. A wife who has never engaged in or
has been unable to enjoy receiving oral sex may tense
when her husband starts to "go down" on her. We have
all kinds of thoughts: *Do I want his mouth on my girly
parts? Is this clean? What do I smell like down there? What
do I look like down there? Eyes up here, buddy; don't look at
my thunder thighs! Does this make me a slut? What does
God think of this? What do I think of this?*

If those are the wife's thoughts (and many more
because our brains are like tidal waves much of the
time), here is what the husband is thinking: *Sex. Wife.
Vulva. Sweet. Love.*

If only we could live in a guy's brain for a minute or
two, we could relax too.

You have to shut off the distractions, train yourself to
open up to the sensations your body is feeling, and go
with the flow. Let your husband turn you on. When
you open your body up to him and to sexual pleasure,
you are beautiful and sexy to him.

How can you help it go well? Learn your body.
Know your anatomy and where stimulation is likely to
feel good. The most pleasurable part of a woman's
anatomy is the clitoris, a knobby bit of flesh at the top
of the genitalia. Doctors and researchers report that this
area must be stimulated directly or indirectly for a

woman to orgasm. But the labia minora are also quite sensitive to touch.

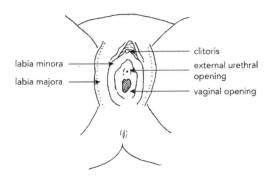

labia minora
labia majora

clitoris
external urethral opening
vaginal opening

As you think about what feels good, give directions. Not as in, "a little to the left, buddy. No, not there! Ouch. Can't you do anything right? The left, the left!" Instead, gently let your husband know what feels good. You can moan, groan, whisper, ooh, ah, talk, gyrate, purr, or even roar—whatever suits your fancy. You can adjust his head so that his lips and tongue contact you in a delightful place. You can use your hand to open up your vaginal lips and give him more direct access. Some wives (and husbands) swear by shaving or waxing that area to increase sensation and arousal; other wives are not comfortable with that. Also, you might want to take a bath or shower beforehand to make sure everything is clean down there and smells nice.

You may wish to talk to your husband ahead of time. Let him know he needs to go slow. It does not feel good to most wives to have hubby go down and start brashly licking or sucking the clitoris. We need time to build up. He can begin by kissing your lips, your body, your thighs, and then move to the genital area. The lips and tongue should be used to tease for a while before pressure is increased. After a while of slow stimulation, you may want him to increase the speed and/or pressure of his mouth's action against your skin.

Will you climax? Maybe. Cunnilingus is one of the easier ways for a woman to experience an orgasm—because the focus is on her and the clitoris can receive direct stimulation. Whether you climax or not, oral sex is likely to feel good to most wives who desire the experience.

Some couples use oral sex as foreplay. In fact, when a wife approaches climax, she may feel a strong desire for penetration. You can allow climax to occur during oral stimulation from your husband or move to intercourse and perhaps experience an orgasm after entry. For women, there are no guarantees for having an orgasm during sexual encounters. In fact, that's not the purpose of marital intimacy. It is about closeness and pleasure. Yet the paradox is that if you focus on your relationship and pleasurable sensations, you are more likely to have that orgasm.

Focus on that pleasure, enjoy the sensations, and delight that your lover wants to please you in that way. You might find that cunnilingus is a great addition to your sexual intimacy.

What if you just don't wanna? If the thought of receiving oral sex sickens you, violates your conscience, or you simply don't enjoy the experience, don't do it. Godly sexuality is never about forcing or demanding sexual acts from your spouse. If you don't want to have oral sex, don't. Find other activities that are mutually pleasurable. The beauty of intimacy in marriage is that, while there are some restrictions, there is a substantial amount of freedom. You can spend the next fifty years getting to know one another's bodies and engaging in physical intimacy that makes your body tingle, your heart pump, and your connection deepen.

Chapter 6
Giving a Hand Job

Have you ever considered how handy your opposable thumbs are for sexual intimacy? Being able to hold, grasp, squeeze, and stroke with our hands is a wonderful aspect of our human bodies. And we wives can even use our hands to bring great pleasure to our husband's manhood.

**"His body is like polished ivory
decorated with lapis lazuli."
Song of Songs 5:10**

How to Give a Hand Job

For many years, I could confidently say that I was a good lover...except when it came to hand jobs. I was downright flummoxed.

Now I can't be the only wife who didn't know how to give her husband a great hand job. But it's good to have this in your marital intimacy repertoire for those times when intercourse is off limits due to a menstrual period or health restrictions or when you merely want some nice foreplay.

So how do you give your husband a great hand job? I have since learned a thing or two.

Lubricant. Rubbing your hand over his penis repeatedly may not feel good without moisture. Grab some lubricant. You can use one that is oil-based (like coconut oil), water-based (like Astroglide or KY), or silicone-based (like Wet Platinum or Sliquid Silver). Find one you both like and start the hand job by applying a reasonable amount to your husband's penis and to your hands. Keep it nearby in case you need more.

Teasing. Take it slow at first. You can take your time undressing your husband and teasing him with your hands outside his clothes or underwear beforehand. Once he's bare, there are several ways to drive him a little crazy with gentle touching: You can touch or lick the head of his penis, lightly massage his testicles, or use your fingers to softly stroke his penis.

Body position. A hand job can be given from several positions. Your husband can sit in a chair while you kneel; he can lie down, while you straddle-sit on his thighs; you can sit next to each other and reach over to touch him; you can lie in opposite directions with your head in line with his hips; and so on and so on. If you have difficulty in one position, try another. Your respective heights and body comfort will make some positions more pleasant and conducive to arousal than others.

The view. Speaking of which, you may want to consider the view he's getting while you're in that body position. Your husband may respond even more to your touching if he's getting a pleasing visual as well. Most men are aroused by seeing their wife's body, in part or in full. While you're giving him the hand job, he may enjoy looking at your breasts, your derrière, or other pretty parts. Or perhaps he simply wants to gaze into your eyes. (*"How beautiful you are, my darling! Oh, how beautiful! Your eyes are doves." Song of Songs 1:15.*)

Hand positions. There are several different ways to position your hands. You can stroke up and down, up only with two hands alternating, twist your hand or hands back and forth around the shaft. You can use your whole hand, your palms only, your fingers, or pinch your finger and thumb together to form a ring (think of the okay sign).

Like sexual positions, some people have named miscellaneous hand job moves, such as "the corkscrew" or "the pancake." But all of them are variations of the grip and stroke you use and the area you touch. There isn't one right hand position for giving a good hand job. As they say, different strokes for different folks. (Now I've ruined that saying for you, haven't I?)

Sensitivity. You may be tempted to concentrate on the shaft of the penis, since constantly stroking it can evoke ejaculation. However, the most sensitive part is the head, or glans, of the penis. Be sure to playfully and lovingly touch your husband's head, paying special attention to the frenulum—which appears like a stretch of taut skin running from the inner head of the penis to the shaft. The corona, or rim of the penis head, is also sensitive to touch.

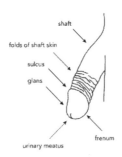

Rhythm. When your husband thrusts inside you, there's a rhythm to it, right? Well, you'll want to maintain a rhythm to your touching. It doesn't have to be consistent throughout; in fact, vary a little. You can start slow, increase the pace, slow again, increase, and so forth. Or just move from slower to faster. But don't stop and start; keep it going.

Climax. Decide how you want to handle ejaculation. Do you two want him to climax with the hand job? Do you want him to penetrate you when he's close? Do you want to maybe add your mouth to the equation and…well, you know? If you want to finish him with the hand job, you'll likely need to increase the pace and pressure as he comes close. You may also want to surround his penis with your whole hand (or two hands) to provide sensation all around for him. Pay attention to his cues: Is he tensing up? Asking for more? Making noises that indicate growing pleasure? Adjust your position and tension accordingly.

One more thing about climax: While it's incredibly enjoyable to most husbands to have their wife fondle and stroke their penis, it's a little more difficult for some husbands to reach orgasm that way. They may prefer to move to penetration or even to take over some of the rhythm with their own hand. This is not a reflection on how good your hand feels to him. You can talk about your expectations here and decide what's important to you both.

Communication. The best advice for giving your husband a fabulous hand job, however, should come from…your husband. He knows what feels good to his body. Encourage him to tell you what he likes or guide your hand(s). Let him know that you want to learn. I bet that statement alone—"Honey, will you show me how to give you a fabulous hand job?"—would cause plenty of husbands to come to attention.

Asking your husband how you can please him falls under one of the foundational principles to a truly intimate and enjoyable physical relationship in your marriage. The Bible's commands are relevant to every area of our lives, including the marital bedroom. So even though it isn't a scripture that addresses sexuality, consider the attitude we should take toward others from Philippians 2:3-4: *"Do nothing out of selfish ambition or vain conceit. Rather, in humility value others above yourselves, not looking to your own interests but each of you to the interests of the others."*

It's a gift to your husband to let go of your selfishness, value his pleasure above your own, and look to his interests. The paradox is that spouses report over and over that their own pleasure increases a hundredfold when they ask how they can serve their mate and then pleasure them accordingly.

Chapter 7
Experiencing an Orgasm

This might be one of the most asked questions: How do I reach that pinnacle of sexual satisfaction? It's certainly the subject of plenty of women's magazine articles. Have you browsed the newsstand lately?

It is true that you will likely enjoy and desire sex more if you can—at least sometimes—experience the physical ecstasy we call "orgasm."

> **"Eat, friends, and drink;**
> **drink your fill of love."**
> **Song of Songs 5:1b**

How to Orgasm

Orgasm. Have you had one? This is an experience many wives desire but struggle to have. It doesn't come easily to everyone. But here are some tips for getting there:

Don't try to orgasm. Yes, it's a worthy goal, and I'm in favor of reaching that awe-inducing climax and yelling "Yippee!" at its apex. However, trying to attain an orgasm is like looking for the perfect shoes. You almost never find them when you're out hunting down what to wear with that outfit you paid too much for. But go out browsing with a girlfriend to enjoy the fun of shopping, and *voilà!* there they are—the perfect shoes practically winking at you through the display window.

Likewise, orgasms are not what you should aim for. Aim instead for pleasure, pleasure, and more pleasure. When the pleasure becomes particularly intense, orgasm occurs. So your target should be enjoying the sex as much as you possibly can.

Learn about your body. There are various approaches to this. Read up on the female body generally. Learn the parts that constitute arousal areas and how they work. The most thorough treatment I've read was from *Intended for Pleasure* by Ed and Gaye

Wheat, but there are other sources. One important fact is that the clitoris is where orgasm occurs for women, and this body part appears to have no other purpose than inducing sexual arousal. (Thank you, God.) The Wheats state that "sufficient physical stimulation of the clitoris alone will produce orgasm in nearly all women." Of course, what constitutes that "sufficient physical stimulation" is what wives, and husbands, need to know.

Some experts suggest that you experiment with your own body, discovering where you like to be touched and with what intensity. It will feel different with your own hand versus your husband's, but this information can be valuable. You can even make this part of a lovemaking session. Most husbands are very aroused by their wives touching themselves, and this can become part of foreplay. It can help him to see what you like.

You can also have your husband explore your body. In this case, I suggest that the wife remove her clothing, but the husband remain dressed for this session (it can be awfully hard for him to not rush in to penetration if he's already naked). Dedicate at least fifteen minutes, but even better a half hour, to him touching you with his hands and lips. It may feel selfish to indulge only one of you, but learning what causes arousal for the wife will benefit the husband in the long run as well.

Slow way down. Men typically do not require as much foreplay as women. In fact, husbands have been compared to microwaves and wives to slow cookers for how long it takes them to heat up. It takes some time for most women to become aroused, fully lubricated, and for the inner vaginal lips (labia minora) to swell.

Moreover, women are mental multi-taskers. This can be a problem when it comes to sex. It takes time to wind down and push the to-do list to the back of our minds; to swat away those pesky distractions rushing through our brains; to relax into the arms of our beloved; to feel valued, treasured, and loved in that moment; and to let go and surrender to the sensations our body is experiencing.

And it's okay that it takes time. It can be a good thing when a wife slows down the lovemaking experience and ensures that a couple basks in the delights of one another. Give the wife time for pleasure and intensity to build.

Focus on the sensations. The female orgasm is mostly mental. As I said, God created females to be multi-taskers, so it's easy for us to think about sex *and*: sex *and* our shopping list; sex *and* the lyrics to the song on the radio; sex *and* the way our breasts sag to the side instead of perking up like we wish they would. But you have to focus on what's happening to your body to give in to it, to enjoy it, to climax.

Make your pleasure almost like meditation. Train yourself to focus on where your husband is touching, kissing, or fondling you. Think intently about your private areas as your husband is pleasuring them. If stray thoughts come in (and they likely will), return your mental gaze to your body and the stimulation of your five senses. Most women must practice this level of concentration—getting rid of distracting thoughts and returning focus to the arousal your body is experiencing. It may take time to do it with ease.

Communicate. Tell him what you like. When something feels particularly good, let your husband know to keep doing it, or have him increase the intensity. When adjustments need to be made, verbally suggest what you want or direct his hands or lips to the area you want aroused.

Can this be awkward? Um, yeah. I've never seen a Hollywood love scene where one actor said to the other, "Oh, not there. Over a little bit. Yeah, right there."

Two things to remember: (1) he wants to pleasure you, so if something else would do more to rev up your engine, he wants to know; (2) he'll respond much better to positive feedback than critical reviews of his performance. For example, rather than saying, "That doesn't feel good," move his hand and say, "I love it when you touch me *there*." Smiles, oohs, ahs, and groans also let a hubby know when he's hit the jackpot. You could throw in a "You rock my world, baby!" if you feel so moved. That usually goes over well.

Surrender to the moment. Orgasm is a paradox of tension and letting go. When a woman feels extreme sexual arousal, her body tenses. But she must surrender to the pleasurable sensations in order for her body to climax. This is something you might practice too. When you start feeling intense pleasure, concentrate on the body part being aroused and relax it. Do this a few times, and see if your pleasure increases.

Give in to the moment when it arrives. Make noises. Grimace. Scream. Flail about. Whatever floats your boat. I wonder about couples who videotape their lovemaking sessions because I'm pretty sure that orgasms are not pretty. If you watched a woman undergoing an intense orgasm, she might look like a rabid animal. But this is not the time to worry about how you look or what the neighbors might think if they heard you. (They're probably thinking "Good for her!") At that apex of pleasure, let go and revel in your one-fleshness.

Multiple and Simultaneous Orgasms

If you currently have orgasms and want to increase the intensity even more, multiples and simultaneous orgasm certainly do that. In particular, having multiple orgasms is enjoyable and delights your husband, while achieving climax together can be a breathtaking, intimate moment for the two of you. But the question is *how?*

MULTIPLE ORGASMS

First of all, it isn't a myth. Quite a few women experience multiple orgasms in a single sexual encounter.

The easiest orgasm to achieve is purely clitoral— meaning that your husband stimulates your clitoris to the point of intense pleasure and eventually that tension releases as a physical wave of spasms and a mental *holy-shivers-that-feels-good* recognition. You know you have had an orgasm when you feel your vagina squeeze and release and your eyes roll to the back of your head and fall onto your pillow. (You can pick them up and return them to your sockets later.) As you can see, I'm rather happy with God giving woman a clitoris, as it has no purpose whatsoever but to provide pleasure for the wife during sex. What a generous God we have!

But wives can also have a vaginal orgasm, which typically occurs with penetration. How can I describe that one? It feels less frenetic and deeper and may last longer. Some experts believe that the key factor for a vaginal orgasm is contact with the G-spot[3]; I'm not sure that's a must. The clitoris is still involved in this orgasm, however, because it receives indirect pressure through thrusting.

Given that not all orgasms are the same, not all multiple orgasms feel the same either. You may have more than one clitoral, a clitoral and a vaginal, more than one vaginal, or whatever. And they will feel different. In fact, clitoral orgasms range as well in their intensity, contractions, feeling of sparks or waves, etc. Which is awesome, ladies! We wives can experience a variety of orgasmic experiences; meanwhile, husbands report that their climaxes are fabulous but pretty straightforward.

As for how to, here are some tips:

Slow, fast, climax, slow, fast, climax, etc. This is particularly true with clitoral orgasms. You can make it a loop. Typically, wives want husbands to go slow for a while and then quicken the pace and increase the

---

[3] The Grafenberg Spot, or G-spot, is an erogenous zone located on the inner wall of the vagina.

pressure. Once a wife has reached the pinnacle of pleasure and achieved orgasm, hubby needs to back down on the pace and pressure. He doesn't need to start over, but since the wife has fallen down the hump in excitement level, she needs to be built up again to reach climax.

Think of it like a roller coaster. The ride inches slowly up to that first peak and then you go careening down the hill with a huge grin and a scream, and then the next hill comes. You have to get up that hill again, and you lose a little speed doing so. But then when you go down that second hill, you're screaming again (*Yippee, this is fun!*). It's slow, fast, slow, fast—or, if you prefer, up, down, up, down.

Clitoral stimulation, then vaginal. Even though a wife can have more than one vaginal orgasm, the clitoral is easier for most women to reach. So I suggest focusing on getting there first, then having the husband enter. To get that second (or ninth, whatever your goal) orgasm, you can do a few things:

Play with sexual positioning. I'm not talking about some contortionist act—just tilt your hips, raise your legs, try woman-on-top, use the edge of the bed to get into an angle that arouses you more or provides deeper penetration, etc.

Have him stimulate other areas of your body. If your breasts are erogenous zones, or having him kiss your neck makes you go crazy, add that extra attention to see if that gets you over the brink.

Continue to stimulate the clitoris while hubby is inside. He can do this with his fingers or, if you are comfortable, you can do it yourself. Most husbands are highly aroused to watch their wives touch themselves. However, you and hubby may wish for him to take charge of this as well. Whatever works for you.

You could also go for a succession of clitoral orgasms and wait on the intercourse longer. Make that decision together to see what you want to do.

If at first you don't succeed... Seriously, don't sweat this. Sex can be very enjoyable for a woman without an orgasm (a brownie). Sex with an orgasm is even better (dollop of ice cream). Sex with multiple orgasms is unnecessary, but rather nice (chocolate sauce). Believe me, if you don't have Hershey's syrup in your cabinet and offer me a brownie and ice cream, I'm still eating and enjoying every bite. You can enjoy it too.

If you don't get wave after wave of awesome orgasm on your first (or fifth) try, keep making love! Try something a little different. Communicate. Experiment. Have fun with it. Ultimately, the best way to know what turns you on the most is not for me to draw a diagram or write an instruction manual (*ignore the irony*), but for you and your husband to explore one another's bodies and sexual responses.

SIMULTANEOUS ORGASM

Reaching orgasm together can be a wonderful experience. Here are my thoughts on that serendipity:

Timing. It's *all* about mastering the timing. If you can each reach climax, then you simply have to figure out who needs to hold off until the other spouse gets there. One spouse must come very close, have patience while the other spouse gets very close, and then knock yourselves out. The ideal simultaneous orgasm is with penetration. It may be easier for some women to have a clitoral orgasm beforehand and then have their husband enter and bring them to climax again. Unlike the guys, we gals can handle a two-fer and the first orgasm may in fact help get a wife to a sexual plateau where it isn't that hard to vault up again into orgasmic pleasure.

Indeed, once you both get very close, one of you having an orgasm will likely help the other get there. That's because the spasms of a wife's orgasm provide pressure on her husband's penis to bring about ejaculation; while the husband's ejaculation will likely cause him to thrust deeper, thus contacting sensitive spots inside a woman that may respond with orgasm.

Luck. You can do some planning with this, but it's my opinion that there is a bit of luck with simultaneous orgasm. Getting the two of you to climax together is a bit like trying to get two runners to cross the finish line at the exact same moment. You can do your best to match another's stride, but breaking that finish line tape together would be difficult to achieve consistently. So take it when it happens, but as a friend of mine said, "This isn't synchronized swimming."

Experience. Couples are better able to climax together when they are older and have been together longer. This is because it is relatively difficult for a young man to postpone climax while an older man can often control his climax better. Additionally, over time sexually-active married couples learn to gauge one another's physical responses and adjust accordingly. At this point in my marriage, no one has to say, "I'm almost there," because the other spouse can tell; we've been there enough to know. Thus, simultaneous orgasm is actually easier to achieve with age and time together. That doesn't mean the young'uns can't get it, but it does mean that if you haven't experienced it yet, you may in the future.

HAVE FUN TRYING

Most women can achieve multiple and simultaneous orgasms at some point in their marriage. However, from a biblical perspective, my experience, and talking with other wives who have had multiples and simultaneous orgasm, the most enjoyable sex comes not from meeting such goals, but from having physical, emotional, and spiritual intimacy in the bedroom.

Seeking these goals in turn helps you reach the physical ones. Feeling comfortable and confident sexually with your husband, being able to explore and communicate with one another during sex, and each having the attitude of pleasuring the other will go a long way toward experiencing multiples and simultaneous orgasm.

Chapter 8
Considering Sexual Positions

*With my odd sense of humor, I am ever so tempted to use
the following quote for this section's intro: "Take your
positions" (Jeremiah 46:4). But since the next part is "Put on
your helmets. Sharpen your spears, and prepare your
armor," that's probably not the right choice.*

*Still, many believe there is a reference to sexual
positioning in the Bible, when the Song of Songs wife twice
refers to the way her husband holds her. And it doesn't sound
like the "missionary position."*

> **"His left arm is under my head
> and his right arm embraces me."
> Song of Songs 2:6 and 8:2**

The Mission for a New Position

I was in the public library once and happened upon the marriage help section. Seeing a title with a couple of Christian authors I recognized, I picked up the book on marital sexuality and thumbed through. Turning to the chapter on positions, I expected to come upon the delicious secrets of sexual positioning, a treasure trove of interesting approaches, a veritable awakening of information regarding the many different ways that a husband and a wife can connect in lovemaking!

There were four positions—described very dryly— all of which my husband and I had done in within our first week or two as newlyweds. Hardly the revelation I was expecting. Sadly, when I mentioned this to a friend of mine, she remarked that three of those positions were probably news to some couples.

Since Christian authors have generally had little to say about positions, many Christian couples turn to the Kama Sutra instead. The Kama Sutra is an ancient Indian Hindu text which includes advice about sexual pleasure and a chapter on positions for coitus. There are 64 positions total.

The Bible's definitive text on godly sexuality does not specifically describe or draw diagrams for sexual positions for married couples. However, scholars do contend that there are clues to positions used by the Lover and Beloved (husband and wife in Song of Songs, or Song of Solomon).

So should a Christian couple pursue different positions? Should they consult other resources? What about those 64 positions? How many of those are worthwhile?

I looked at resources, including Kama Sutra books, the Song of Songs, websites, and conversations with very close friends.[4] And my hubby and I tried some of them. Having done some research and experimentation, let me share what I've discovered.

There are only a few main positions, but many variations. For instance, the missionary position (lying down, man on top, woman on bottom, face-to-face) is one category. Within that category, the way it feels for both partners can be varied—depending on where you place your legs, feet, arms, etc. Rear entry (a husband entering his wife's vagina from behind) is another category, but how much you bend your body and where you place your hands provides different sensations. Those 64 positions in the Kama Sutra? They are really variations within a few major categories.

---

[4] I don't consult secular sources which use photographs as instructional material, since using a resource that has paid two people to pose in sexual positions for an audience is not God-honoring in my book. I don't get sex ideas from hard porn or soft porn.

Some positions are unrealistic. I agree completely with an excellent blog post from Julie Sibert of *Intimacy in Marriage* titled "Hey, I'm a Housewife, Not a Gymnast." Some of the positions out there require a contortionist or a willingness to undergo traction later to perform. And for the husband, let's just say that some things don't bend the way that certain pictures indicate. If any man can do the position I once saw depicted in a diagram in which the hubby is in a back bend, he should consider trying out for the Olympic Gymnastics Team or Cirque du Soleil. That one is definitely not happening for most couples.

Varying positions provides several benefits.

Visual stimulation. Seeing you and your spouse connected from different perspectives can be titillating. For instance, woman-on-top may be particularly appealing for a husband to view his wife's beautiful body.

Access. Certain positions provide better access to body parts that you want to touch or kiss. Perhaps one time the wife wishes to stroke her husband's testicles by sitting atop him or the husband wants to enter from the rear to more easily fondle his wife's breasts.

Control. You may wish to vary who has more control over the time of entry, thrusting, and pacing. At times, the wife may want to have more say for when she is ready for penetration—which may be easier for her from above. Other times, the husband may wish to assume charge.

Sensation. The husband penetrating his wife from different angles provides different sensations. For instance, rear entry may be more comfortable for wives with a severely tilted, or retroverted, uterus. Also, certain positions have a greater chance of engaging the ever-elusive G-spot (though some couples never find it and enjoy sex just fine).

It's okay to be adventurous, and it's okay to not be adventurous. Not every position is worth trying, and positioning alone is *not* the secret to having a great sex life. Spending your time developing a loving, intimate relationship with your husband is much more worthwhile than reading through the Kama Sutra or any other sex manual. Don't go making a list of all 64 positions with a box to check off beside each one.

The best way to start is to vary your regular position(s) a little. Move your arms or legs somewhere else. Tilt a little to the left or right. Angle yourselves a bit differently. Involve a chair or the side of the bed to create slightly different positioning.

Mission Position isn't about trying everything so you can say that you've done it all. It's about one key to a great sex life with your husband: Loving them enough to find ways to mutually experience physical pleasure. If changing up your positioning increases your enjoyment of one another, go for it! If you're both unbelievably ecstatic with that one perfect position you've got going, keep going. If your husband wants to try something new and you're reluctant, you might end up enjoying it after all if you gave it a try.

Trying Positions

Yet another time, I was in a secondhand bookstore perusing the shelves and, as often happens these days, ended up in the sexuality section. (I like to see what's published and read on this topic, especially books by Christian authors.) On this visit, I picked up a book on sexual positions, which included a drawing of a woman in a back bend and the man thrusting into her.[5]

I'd previously seen a drawing of a man in a back bend with the woman on top.

Who does that? Circus people? I was both intrigued and alarmed that anyone would get into that position to have sex.

That said, there are a lot of sexual positions worth trying. Some provide more access to view each other, some provide more control for one partner or the other, and some provide different sensations. So let's say you want to try a new sexual position. How do you know what to try? Besides a back bend (heaven, help us all), what are the options?

What I've figured out is that all of those positions suggested in books (like the 64 positions of the Kama Sutra) are really variations on a theme.

First, there is relative positioning.

<u>Man on top</u>. Face-to-face, husband on top.

<u>Woman on top</u>. Also face-to-face but wife on top.

<u>Side by side</u>. A couple facing each other side by side.

<u>Rear entry</u>. Husband entering wife's vagina from behind.

Next, there is general positioning.

<u>Lying down</u>. Husband and wife are mostly lying down.

<u>Kneeling</u>. One or both are on your knees.

<u>Sitting</u>. The wife sits on her husband's lap.

<u>Standing</u>. Both husband and wife standing up.

Third, there is the angle of your torso and limbs— mainly wife.

<u>Crouched</u>. Your torso is bent. For a wife, this usually means bending at the waist to create a shorter distance between entry and the end of her vagina. Bending in this way can increase the likelihood of her husband thrusting into her elusive G-spot.

<u>Spread wide</u>. The wife spreads her legs wide which gives the best access for viewing, touch, and entry. In this position, the husband may be able to go deeper into her vagina as well.

<u>Legs together</u>. When a wife keeps her legs together, it can create greater friction on the man's penis and squeeze the opening a bit to provide more pressure.

---

[5] I avoid sex books with photography to illustrate.

Legs bent. One or both legs can be bent just slightly, moderately, or with the wife's knees all the way up to her chest. Each configuration provides a different sensation to both the husband and wife. In particular, the knees-to-chest position can feel more intense and allow the penis to brush against the wife's G-spot.

Legs up. Throwing your legs up in the air may feel awkward at first, but lifting the legs changes the angle of the body as well. A wife can even drape her legs over her husband's shoulders.

You can come up with all kinds of positions by simply playing mix-and-match here. Let me show you what I mean.

Mix and match.

So here's your typical sexual position: Man on top, lying down, spread wide.

Now here's man on top, standing, legs up.

How about woman on top, sitting, legs bent?

Rear entry, kneeling, legs together?

You see what I mean? You can achieve numerous positions just with these basics.

Also, wives, tilting your hips is another way to shift the angle and feel something different. For example, in that last position, the wife can move her chest toward the bed or ground and tilt her hips up to meet her husband. In the missionary position, she can tilt her hips up off the bed.

If you've never tried anything adventurous in this area, start small. Keep the other two positions as usual and change the third. For instance, keep direction and general position and change the angle. Or keep direction and angle and change general position. You get the idea.

By the way, many scholars believe that Song of Songs 2:6 is a reference to a sexual position: *"His left arm is under my head, and his right arm embraces me."* It sounds like side by side to me, but it certainly doesn't appear to be the missionary position (man on top). So I guess the Lover and the Beloved were a little adventurous themselves.

Chapter 9
Choosing Location

Have you ever wondered where Adam and Eve made love? There's no master bedroom mentioned in Genesis.

As attached as we've gotten to our locked bedroom doors and cushy mattresses, there are plenty of other options for where a married couple can have sex. Let's explore the pros and cons of various locations.

"Let us go early to the vineyards to see if the vines have budded,
if their blossoms have opened, and if the pomegranates are in bloom —
there I will give you my love."
Song of Songs 7:12

Where Not to Have Sex

At times it seems that we married people are an unimaginative lot. After all, most of have 99% of our sex in—*can you guess?*—a bed.

One suggestion for introducing a little playfulness, creativity, or adventure into your sex life is to vary where you have sex. Location, location, location. Besides atop the king mattress set, where else can a husband and wife be intimate? In the spirit of the medical ethics principle of Primum non nocere ("First, do no harm"), let's focus on…

Places you *think* would be fun for sex, but in reality, not so much.

Elevator. The thought of being alone in an elevator with your hubby, stripping down, and doing it against the wall or on the floor as you go up or down sounds adventurous. In fact, there seems to be a lot of innuendo, making out, and sex going on in elevators in the movies. There is even an Aerosmith song, "Love in an Elevator."

However, many elevators these days have cameras. So unless you're trying to entertain the security guard with a free porn movie, why go there? Plus, if you push the Stop button on an elevator, someone might call for help, and you may be preventing someone from getting someplace they need to go. Finally, are you putting a plastic cover down, or messing up their carpet? I'm just sayin'.

Think of this: An elevator is simply a moving closet. If you want that experience, put full length mirrors along the walls of your closet, install a handrail, pipe in some easy listening tunes, and pretend to push the Lobby button. Same thing, no photographic evidence.

Beach. Remember that great scene in *From Here to Eternity* in which Burt Lancaster and Deborah Kerr roll around on the beach in each other's arms and everyone thinks, *Wow*. The sun's rays beating down, the waves licking your bodies, the wind blowing through your hair. Could it get any sexier?

Now for the reality of sexual activity on the beach: Sand gets everywhere. And I mean *everywhere*. If you think the worst place to pick grains of sand from is your ear canal, you are sadly mistaken. Throwing down a blanket won't stop that wonderful wind from blowing the sand your way. Plus, there are birds. You do not want a flock of seagulls watching you mate or dropping their souvenirs on your head.

Kitchen table. Another movie-inspired idea, I think. Thanks to Kevin Costner and Susan Sarandon in *Bull Durham*, it's appealing to a lot of women to imagine the husband clearing off a table and taking her right then, right there. This could also be a desk, as many have imagined making love at one or the other's workplace.

Newsflash! Tables and desks are hard. It is not comfortable to have your hips, back, derrière, etc. slammed against a surface with as little give as a concrete sidewalk. Positioning yourself for intercourse is not always easy, and if your back and knees are over 30 years old, grab the pain reliever before you even begin.

Ground. Mosquitoes, chiggers, and ants, o my! If you lay your naked bodies down right on the dirt or grass, you can expect to make contact with nature. Sometimes nature is beautiful; sometimes it is harsh. You do not want to have an orgasm followed by poison ivy in the same place. Even if the sex is fabulous, is it worth scratching your nether regions for two weeks? Of course, this is preventable with a little planning.

Bring a quilt, a blanket, or at least a tarp. Put something between you and God's green earth. Yes, I know that the Song of Songs speaks of the married couple being in the vineyard and under the apple tree, but I imagine that smart chap having a bed linen at the ready.

Church parking lot. Several years ago, someone left used condoms in our church parking lot. Very uncool. I had to get a latex glove and paper towels, grab the icky prophylactic, and trash it before a child could pick it up and ask, "What's this?" The offending party probably should not have been having sex to begin with (assuming that was fornication), but even if he was married, he could have chosen a more conducive location.

In reality, any place where children are present and could see you or your evidence is not an appropriate location for sex. There's a reason why people advise, "Get a room."

In the next chapter, I'll give a few suggestions of great places to have sex that don't involve a bed.

Where to Try Having Sex

As I mentioned in the previous chapter, one of the ways to spice up your marital intimacy is by changing up your location.

There's a reason why we so often choose our bed as the place to have sex. It's comfortable. There's a flexible mattress, cushy pillows, cool sheets, warm blankets, and plenty of space. However, there are other options besides the bed, an elevator, the beach, the table, and—heaven forbid—a port-a-john (a terrible location one blog reader mentioned). I'm all in favor of varying the location to introduce a little spice into the experience.

Outside. Wait! Wasn't that on my no-no list? Yes, but here's the thing: The outdoors can be a beautiful setting for lovemaking, and the feel of a breeze on your skin can heighten arousal with your lover. The trick is to pick your outdoor location with care. You do not want to find yourself naked among the ant beds or poison ivy. Head to your backyard (assuming it's fenced), your porch or deck, or find another private outdoor location. If you have a playground structure or tree house in your yard, try that. Bring a blanket or quilt and let the moon provide the mood lighting and the birds, crickets, and cicadas provide the music. You could also set up a tent in your yard and camp out together.

Vehicle. Well, it depends on the vehicle. Those of you who drive a Smart Car should put this one in last chapter's "not so much" category. Also if you're in a classic Corvette, you'll find the stick shift gets in the way. In the United States, however, vehicles have gotten larger and larger, so if you're driving a van, an SUV, or a truck, you likely have ample room to get it on in the back seat or truck bed. Find an out-of-the-way location or even your garage, pack a romantic picnic, and turn on your car radio. Turn off the vehicle's engine and rev up your own engine. Pretty soon, it'll be humming and purring with delight. Steaming up the windows and shaking the car are added bonuses to this activity.

Chair in your house. A chair is not a bed. But find a cushioned chair nonetheless, not a hardback wooden one. A chair is a great place to vary your intimacy routine because there are sexual positions you can get into with the assistance of a chair that are not easily done on a bed. The wife can sit on her husband's lap facing forward or straddle him facing the back of the chair. The couple can use the chair for leverage or kneeling. You could also use a bench seat for the same purpose.

Explore and figure out what works as a couple. Just use your imagination.

Water. By water, I mean any place where there is water: your shower, your bath, a hot tub, a river, the ocean, a pool…you get the idea. And by sex, I mean the whole kit-and-caboodle, not just intercourse. Adding a little H20 to the lovemaking can be a scintillating experience. The shower, pool, etc. is a fabulous place for foreplay, but not for penetration. It's difficult to get into a good position, surfaces are slippery, and water can wash away the necessary moisture for comfortable entry.

But go ahead and get naked and explore one another's bodies. Kiss and fondle. Lick and grope. There is something about the water against your skin that can enliven your senses and make you even more responsive to your spouse's touch. When you're ready for more, move the party to a more conducive location for lovemaking.

Cozy rug or blanket. I'm not talking about a scratchy oriental rug that you bought at a garage sale and never cleaned. Or your childhood Holly Hobbie Quilt. I'm talking about a soft fabric placed on the floor—maybe in front of a fireplace or covered with rose petals and lit with candles. Aaaaah, inviting.

Homemade fort. Just like you did as a kid, build a sheets-and-blankets fort and decorate it however you want. Make it your love den. Then climb inside and get going.

Boat. Actually, I don't know if a boat is a good place to have sex. It's just on my list of "I'd like to try it." It seems like you'd need a big enough one to stay steady in the water, but a gentle rocking motion might be nice too.

Change up the location and see if that spices up your experience. If nothing else, you'll have that shared memory of "Remember when we…"?

Chapter 10
Using Your Body Parts

Sex should involve so much of our bodies, as we touch, kiss, and join together in this intimate act to express and foster love. So let's discuss how to use your various body parts in lovemaking: your mouth, your arms, your legs, your hips, etc.

**"The wife does not have authority over her own body but yields it to her husband.
In the same way, the husband does not have authority over his own body but yields it to his wife."
1 Corinthians 7:4**

First, Your Mind

When it comes to using your body for marital intimacy, let's cover first things first. While some husbands might assert that the notion of sex begins somewhere between your belt buckle and your kneecaps, we wives know that sex begins in the mind. That's the body part we ladies need to get into the groove so that we can…well, get into the groove.

Unfortunately, we mental multi-taskers often have difficulty focusing on sexual intimacy with our husbands. It might not seem like such a tall order, but setting aside all of the other thoughts and concentrating solely and wholly on lovemaking can be a challenge for many wives.

So how can we involve our mind in sexual intimacy?

Set aside the time and space. Start by making sure external distractions are not competing. Yes, there are times when you must squeeze sex into eight minutes flat while your toddler is finishing his nap or you shove work piles from the bed to make love, but that shouldn't be the norm.

Set aside time on your calendar or in your schedule. Make it a priority somewhere below breathing or eating and way above a pedicure or polishing faucet fixtures. When you set your mind to spending the next

30 minutes in physical intimacy with your husband, you can more freely engage without thinking of everything else you could be doing.

Also set aside space so that you two have room to make love without the distractions of children's toys, electronics, to-do lists, etc. Remove from your sight and mind whatever might compete for your attention.

Start anticipating in advance. Think ahead of time about how you will feel in the arms of your beloved. Be positive in your anticipation—considering how your senses will be awakened, how your husband's touch will comfort and arouse you, how you want to pleasure him and be pleasured, how precious this gift of sexual union is.

Some wives anticipate sex with dread, ranking it alongside toilet cleaning in their daily task list. If you experience pain or have no drive, you need to address those issues. But our brains are very powerful, so if you simply don't look forward to the experience, retrain your mind. Choose to focus your mental energy on those lovemaking moments that were enjoyable and anticipate that you can have that pleasure once again. The more you joyfully approach an event, the more likely you are to enjoy it.

Focus on your hubby. See that hottie over there? Yep, that one: your hubby. That's the guy you chose (and who chose you). You must've thought he was something special when you said "I do," so dwell on what's so great about your husband.

Think about the physical and internal attributes that are attractive to you. Drop the negative stuff from your mind. Of course, he's annoying at times; my husband is too. (Guess what? We annoy them back.) This is the time to pull your mind toward the beauty of his body, the strength of his character, the fun he brings to life, the gift of his love.

Consider how you desire your husband and how you want him to rejoice in you and be captivated by your love (Proverbs 5:18-19). Keep your mind actively engaged in thinking about your husband and lover.

Become aware of your own body. Your body is equipped with five incredible senses and an amazing number of skin receptors that register touch, temperature, vibration, pressure, and more. On top of that, God blessed certain parts of your body with extra sensitivity to respond happily to sexual arousal. Indeed, one part of your body, the clitoris, has absolutely no purpose whatsoever but to make you giddy with delight when appropriately stimulated.

When making love with your husband, turn your mind to the sensations your body is experiencing. Think about the places he touches, kisses, fondles, strokes, penetrates. If you mind begins to wander to whether you turned off the oven or how much you distrust Congress or whatever, regain control and return your mind to where it should be—on the interesting tickles and tingles of your body.

Also think about how your body can produce delightful feelings for your husband. Your hands, lips, breasts, and other parts of your body have the amazing ability to bring him great pleasure. Revel in how he feels against that hand, those lips, those breasts, etc.

Turn your mind to gratitude. Gratitude is an attitude nurtured in the mind. God has given married couples the gift of sexual intimacy. He could have made it simply for reproduction, but our Father wanted us to enjoy sex and use it to grow intimacy. What a gift!

Just as you pause to soak in the beauty of a colorful sunset or the melodious sounds of your favorite song, pause in your mind to be grateful for sexual intimacy. Make it a regular habit to thank God and your mate for your sexual pleasure.

Begin with the mind, and then embark on the wonderful journey of your bodies coming together in marital intimacy.

What to Do with Your Hands

Did you know that if you type the keyword "hands" into a Bible search engine, you get 579 results. "Hand"? 748 results. "Touch"? Only 40.

Yet I scanned every one of those 1367 verses mentioned above, with help from the Holy Spirit and caffeine, to see what the Bible had to say.

There wasn't much. Well, there is Zephaniah 3:16b: ". . . *do not let your hands hang limp.*"

Just kidding. That verse has nothing to do with sex (even if it is good advice).

Yet hands represent several important concepts in the Bible, such as:

- possession (e.g., one nation given into the hands of another)
- power (e.g., "by His mighty hand"; David's hand killing Goliath)
- skill (e.g., the work of one's hands)
- presence (e.g., God's hand with someone)
- reverence (e.g., lifting hands in prayer)
- importance (e.g., sitting at one's right hand)
- tenderness (e.g., Jesus touching those he healed)

All of these could apply to marriage. For instance, the only one who gets to put hands on our girly parts is the hubster. (Okay, gynecologists too, but let's not digress, ladies, to the uncomfortable memory of our last Pap smear.) The point is that hubby and I put our hands on each other because *"My beloved is mine, and I am his" (Song of Songs 2:16).* Possession.

We can also convey power, skill, presence, reverence (for the Creator of the human body), importance, and tenderness when we touch each other. All good things in marriage.

But let's look specifically at HOW to touch your mate. These are general tips, so see what works for your husband.

Teasing. Typically, you want to use the tips of your fingers or fingernails and work slowly across his skin. Go back and forth, work in circles, or trace your name or a message. Start with less erotic areas and work toward the Big Kahuna.

And here's an interesting trick: Run your fingers along his skin at the edge of his clothing. It doesn't matter whether it's his shirt sleeve or the edge of his underwear, there's something about teasing along that border that is all kinds of sexy.

Stroking. To stroke is to rub or caress, meaning that your hubby should now feel your hand substantially touching him. Use your fingers for a lighter touch or your whole hand for more intensity.

Where should you stroke? Anywhere he wants. But try these sensitive male areas: his neck, his scalp, his ears, his lower abdomen, his inner thighs. He probably has greater sensitivity anywhere that hair isn't— including backs of knees and inside elbows—but those spots depend on your hubby. Of course, if you want a super-charged reaction, move up from that inner thigh to his penis and get to stroking there.

Massaging. Raise your hand if a back rub has ever turned into a lovemaking session you didn't plan. Yeah, us too. But if you add massage to the plan, you'll likely enjoy the results.

Work with just your hands or add lotion or massage oil for easier movement. Make sure the pressure feels good to your man. Usually guys prefer greater pressure, but not always. (I usually beg my husband to massage my poor muscles harder, while he prefers a lighter touch.) You can rub with your thumbs, fingers, the heel of your hand, palms, knuckles, etc., but engage your entire hands in one way or another during the massage.

To keep it sensual, start with hubby on his stomach. Progress something like this:

Neck & shoulders –> back & arms –> length of his spine –> calves –> feet –> back to thighs –> buttocks.

Then flip that relaxed man over and get creative.

Grabbing. Most wives don't want to be cooking and suddenly feel their husband's hand squeezing one butt cheek. But men? They tend to desire more intensity in their wife's touch. Your hubby may think it's super-hot for you to walk up, plant your hand over that rarely-used undies flap, and give his little guy a pump or two. That's a cue that can't easily be missed, and he might appreciate a clear signal that you're good-to-go.

During sex, increasing your grip to the level of grabbiness (is that word?) can let your mate know that you're edging up the excitement meter. You can grab his shoulders, wrap your hands around the back of his head, or sink your hands into his backside and give a good squeeze. Or maneuver him into positions that feel particularly good, like grabbing his buttocks to pulling him deeper into you.

Touching yourself. Most husbands enjoy watching their wives touch themselves. Why? It's a visual thing. Plus, they get up-close-and-personal tutoring on what turns you on so they can mimic those motions later and get you all hot and bothered with their own hands.

If you've never done this before, it's going to feel weird the first time. And probably the second. Let's face it: Your hand and his hand do not feel the same. Also, having an audience, even if it's only your husband, can make it hard to relax and become aroused.

Be willing to start slow—teasing and stroking yourself like discussed above—and then move to your breasts and vulva. You may want to add lubrication down below.

After that, tune in to what your body wants—be it slow and soft touches or faster movement and increased pressure. If you want to achieve orgasm as he watches, find that knobby bit of flesh above your vagina (your clitoris) and stroke it gently, moving in various ways to see what feels good. Increase speed and pressure as you heat up. For tips on reaching orgasm, check out the chapter on that topic.

Adding touch to intercourse. Your hands can also boost stimulation during intercourse. As your husband thrusts, stroke the lower part of his penis, tenderly caress his testicles, or rub your own clitoris or breasts. Any of these may add to the arousal you two experience.

Hand jobs. Of course, you can also perform the aptly-named hand job. For tips, see the chapter on hand jobs.

This is by no means a comprehensive rundown on what you can do with your hands. But I wasn't sure if I should provide a primer here on how to claw your husband's back when you're in the throes of passion. Sure, you can do it, but it's not really a planned thing.

Use your imagination to expand on the ideas here. Just keep your hands involved in the sexual encounter.

By the way, the one biblical passage specifically about hands and sex comes from—no surprise—Song of Songs: *"My beloved thrust his hand through the latch-opening; my heart began to pound for him. I arose to open for my beloved, and my hands dripped with myrrh, my fingers with flowing myrrh, on the handles of the bolt"* (5:4-5). But their hands aren't even touching the other yet, just anticipating when they will. Which can still be arousing.

Closing up my chapter on using your hands in marital intimacy, let's finish with one more verse about the fabulous hand. Ecclesiastes 9:10a says, *"Whatever your hand finds to do, do it with all your might . . ."* Can I get an "Amen"?

What to Do with Your Mouth

As with hands, I started with the Bible and looked up all the passages I could find that included the words mouth, lips, tongue, and kiss. (Yes, I have a very interesting search history.) Then I did some other research, some of it hands-on (because that's just how dedicated I am to helping you).

Following are tips for how to use your mouth in marital lovemaking:

Speak lovingly. We might as well start here, since the vast majority of the passages with mouth, lips, or tongue relate to what we say. The Bible emphasizes again and again the importance of measuring our words and using them responsibly. Now I can't be the only one who learned this verse while watching VeggieTales's "Larry Boy and the Rumor Weed": *"Reckless words pierce like a sword, but the tongue of the wise brings healing" (Proverbs 12:18).* (Thanks, Larry Boy!) And that's a great summary scripture: Words matter.

The lovers in Song of Songs totally got this. Just read a few chapters and see how the spouses speak of and to each other to get examples. The words you speak during lovemaking can tear down your husband or make him feel desired, loved, and adept as a lover.

Consider how your mouth can be used to speak words that build up your hubby and your marital intimacy. Then speak 'em!

Pucker up. The first full sentence in the Song of Songs is: *"Let him kiss me with the kisses of his mouth—for your love is more delightful than wine."* That's a perfect way to start your sexual encounter, using that mouth for some delicious kissing.

Of course, you can join lips to lips, mouth to mouth, and tongue to tongue, but you can also kiss almost anywhere on his body. Now of course, I am not planning to ever kiss my husband's armpit, but I'd say that 98% of your man's body would love to feel the touch of your lips. And some places may respond particularly well to the soft, wet touch of a kiss. Try a few of these:

His eyelids. Yep, eyelids. They're surprisingly sensitive, and kissing his eyelids means he must close his eyes, which can heighten the sense of touch.

His ears. Kiss those lobes, up the curve of his ear, and behind his ear. Some guys go a little crazy with such kisses.

His neck and collarbone. Nuzzle right in there under his chin and get busy. Move your lips up, down, and all around…and work your way down to his collarbone, which is also sensitive for most men.

His nipples. You're not the only one with sensitive nipples. Maybe his aren't quite so much, but they might still enjoy your mouth hanging out there a bit.

His stomach. Tease your kisses all over his tummy, giving some extra attention around his navel.

His thighs. Maybe it's the proximity to where he'd really like your mouth to be, but your hubby's thighs are likely an erogenous zone. Especially the inner thigh. Move your mouth around in gentle kisses and see if he likes it. (If I were a betting woman, I'd put down a fiver that he will.)

His butt. Yes, ladies, I'm talking butt. It's the flipside of his Happytown, and it wouldn't mind your mouth going up and down its hills.

His penis. Indeed, the mayor of Happytown would love a visit from your lips. Shaft, head, frenulum — wherever you're willing to lay your lips. Also, his testicles are sensitive to your touch, whether by hands or mouth. But be extra gentle there!

His hands. You didn't expect me to go from the penis to something so seemingly ho-hum as his hands. But our hands are very sensitive, and you can turn him on by kissing his hands, especially the inside of his palm.

Lick it up. So sue me for quoting KISS (not the pucker-up, the rock band). But honestly, your tongue is a lovely tool for arousal. You can lick any of the places mentioned above.

Be gentle with your tongue in most of these spots. You can use the tip of your tongue to tease and titillate. Think how you might lick an envelope. To give a more intense experience, flatten out your tongue and go at your husband like he's a dripping ice cream scoop. Go slow to draw out the sensation. Of course, you can also flick your tongue, moving the tip up-and-down or side-to-side.

Nibble. One of the Google definitions for nibble is to "gently bite at (a part of the body), esp. amorously or nervously." Let's go with amorously.

I didn't look up teeth in the Bible, but they're in your mouth and they're awfully handy for a providing a stronger touch and a little tug on your husband's flesh. How hard you bite is up to him. Pay attention to his reaction. Some husbands would welcome a little chomp-down on the shoulder or a strong tug on the earlobe. Other hubbies are more sensitive and would rather you focus on the word *gently* in that definition of nibble.

But wait, don't bite his manly stuff down there! You do want them to survive another day, right?

Suck, the good way. When my husband annoys me and I want to jokingly let him know, my typical statement is "You suck...and not in the good way." Which gets both of us laughing (and sometimes a little turned-on) and defuses any tension that might have been there. But I'm hitting at something true: sucking is a nice piece of your mouth's lovemaking repertoire.

Now don't go all "vacuum" on him; you're not Hoover. But put your mouth on him and pull your mouth together in a nice, long, gentle suck. Most of those places—now listed way back there—are fair game, but a few other spots are suck-worthy. When you kiss together, you can suck on his lips a little. You can also take each of his fingers and pull them into your mouth for a little sucking. And for a big reaction, suck on his top part of his penis, paying special attention with your tongue to the stretch of flesh that connects the shaft with the head on the lower side (the frenulum).

Once your mouth has given pleasure to your husband, let's hope his response is like that of the lover in Song of Songs:

"Your lips drop sweetness as the honeycomb, my bride; milk and honey are under your tongue" (4:11).

Use these tips to do something you haven't done yet or to revisit something you haven't done in a while. Just think about the wonder of God's gift of your mouth in providing pleasure to your spouse. There are so many ways you can use it.

What to Do with Your Legs

In Song of Songs 7:1, the husband comments on his wife's lovely gams, *"Your graceful legs are like jewels, the work of an artist's hands."*

But beyond being a beautiful part of the body for him to gaze upon, what can you do with your legs during lovemaking with your husband? For ease, I am defining "legs" here as everything from just below your hip down, including your feet.

Touch. You can start by stroking your husband with your legs and/or feet. When you embrace, rub your legs against his legs or torso. Stroke his back or buttocks with your calves or feet. Wrap your legs around his body. Skin-to-skin contact heightens arousal. Often the more your bodies touch, the better. So involve your legs and feet in touching your man.

You can also use your feet to rub his testicles or his penis. Be gentle! It's a bit harder to control the pressure of your touch with feet than hands, so you'll need to be careful to touch the jewels delicately, please. But playing "footsie" with his privates could be a big turn-on for your hubby.

Proximity. Your legs are a great way to signal to your husband how close you want him to be. Assuming you're making love face-to-face, you can wrap your legs around his body and pull him in closer with your legs. This is especially useful when he's thrusting and you want him to go deeper.

Of course, your legs can also push him away. For instance, if you want a break to change position, you can use your feet or legs to push him back and reposition your body.

Sexual positioning. So here's the biggie. Your legs can play a starring role in sexual positioning with your husband. Besides the usual on-the-bed placement, or wrapped around your honey, what can you do with your legs to try different positions?

Legs wide. This may seem obvious, but there are times when you should spread particularly wide—that is, send one leg east and the other west. For instance, to give your husband a clear view of your private beauty, to provide easy access for oral sex, or to experience a different sensation during intercourse.

Legs together. Closing your legs tighter can provide more pressure on the hubs and provide an interesting sensation for you. This can be done from a front-to-front position, with him behind, spooning, or several other basic positions. The closeness of your thighs-to-knees is what matters.

Legs raised. Positioning your legs and feet up either behind your husband or on him can affect how sexual intercourse feels. Changing your legs' position changes the angle at which your genitals connect, meaning that the sensations you experience can change. And you may find a position you like particularly well.

What do I mean by "raised"? Options include placing your legs over his shoulders, keeping your legs up and straight, bending your legs and placing your feet on his chest. You can also do these positions while sitting in a chair or, for the adventurous, standing.

Those are some choices you have, but you can move your legs here, there, and wherever to create different angles. Changing up your legs' position can provide different visuals, access, and sensations for you both. Experiment and see how it feels.

Rhythm. Your legs, knees, and feet can also control or contribute to the rhythm of your lovemaking. For instance, by squatting over your husband's body, the wife can take control of the thrusting herself, using up-and-down and rocking motions. In a hands-and-knees position, with the husband entering the vagina from behind, the wife can also rock her body on her legs and meet the rhythm that he provides. The wife can also put her feet on his chest, against the wall behind her husband, or on the floor if they're sitting to get some traction for using her legs and pulsing her body against his.

If you've left the thrusting entirely to your husband thus far, I suspect he'd love to see you get involved.

Use those legs and move against him in a way that shows you're a happy participant. You might also like taking charge at times, so that you can adjust to what feels good to you and increase your pleasure. (Which will likely increase his pleasure, since the vast majority of husbands are very aroused seeing their wife aroused.)

What to Do with Your Hips

Look up "hip" in your Bible, and there isn't much in the way of romance. There is mention of how the behemoth's strength is in his hips (Job 40:17), but if a husband dared to bring that reference into the bedroom, he'd deserve the glacier-melting glare he got from his wife.

Interestingly enough, in the two passages in Song of Songs where the husband describes the beauty of his wife's body (chapters 4 and 7), he skips right over the pelvic area. Legs are described. Waist is described. But not what comes in between, even though it's a rather important part of the whole deal. Instead, the Lover (husband) primarily refers to his wife's lady parts with symbolic language, such as "garden."

But the way God designed a woman's hips allows them to be somewhat of a wonder worker in sexual intimacy with her husband. If she knows how to use them.

Using your hips in marital intimacy can be described by the kinds of motions you can make with them.

Tilting. Front-to-back, your hips can work like a pendulum. Tilting them toward your husband can alter the angle of entry and the resulting sensations you both feel. It can also signal to him that you are fully engaged in what's happening.

When making love face-to-face, you can tilt your hips forward, which may allow your husband to move deeper. In the rear entry position (husband entering his wife's vagina from behind), tilting your hips backward opens up the area for him to engage more fully.

Rocking. With that same pendulum motion, you can rock your hips forward and backward. This is one of the ways that a wife can take control of some of the thrusting. It is easiest done with the woman-on-top position, where she can pulse her hips in a consistent rhythm.

Altering the speed of rocking can affect whether this is a playful motion that draws out lovemaking or a more intense motion that draws toward climax. Advantages of this position and motion are that the husband has a wonderful view of his wife's body and he can continue to touch her breasts and clitoris to increase her pleasure.

Wiggling. Wiggling seems the appropriate word for this motion, because it's kind of like fidgeting your hips around in your chair—only on your husband. This is a sort of tease you can do with your hips and can be very enjoyable as you pay attention to the way your body parts connect and alter slightly with each movement.

Be careful not to wiggle too much or too fast, since his erect penis is not meant to be that flexible.

Riding. Oh, how I considered and reconsidered this descriptive word! But that's really what it is. If you've ever been on a horse (or an elephant or a camel—whatever you ride), you know that feeling of your hips bouncing up and down as the animal trots or gallops.

That same up-and-down bouncing motion can be incredibly hot during sex. The wife moves her hips straight up and down, creating the rhythmic thrust for making love. She does the work, but she's also more in control of her pleasure. If needed, she can slow down the pace to draw out her arousal, perhaps increasing the likelihood that she can achieve climax along with her husband during intercourse. Her husband can also signal what he desires by placing his hands outside her hips and guiding her.

Honestly, the best way to "ride" is to plant your feet (think back to the way an equestrian has stirrups to steady her feet). Thus, squatting over your husband will allow more control than kneeling. Your knees and hips can act together to provide that up-and-down motion. If your legs tire, you can change positions to kneeling for a bit and then return to squatting...or at this point, you might agree to have your husband simply flip you over and take charge (because he's likely very turned on by how active you are in this sexual encounter).

There you go—ways to use your hips in marital intimacy.

Heart and Soul

While I believe that marriages can benefit from specific coaching and tips (or I wouldn't have bothered to write this book), I don't believe technique is as important as other factors. It's quite possible for both participants to be technically fabulous lovers and not experience fulfilling sexual intimacy.

How do I know this? Okay, sadly, I know this because I've had both experiences. What is the biggest difference between my premarital sexual encounters and my marital sexual encounters? The former attempted to have meaning (and failed), but the latter has deep, deep meaning.

Why? Because my marital intimacy is born of an entirely different relationship: one that involves committed, covenant love; years of shared sorrows, joys, tears, and laughter; security and hope for our future; and the blessing of our Heavenly Father. For sexual intimacy to be the full gift that God intends it to be, it must involve the heart and soul of husband and wife.

The Song of Songs (or Song of Solomon) describes the beautiful sexual love between a husband and a wife. The passages are romantic, passionate, and—if you read 'em right—can be titillating. But in the last chapter, we get a clear picture of what makes their sexual love so meaningful. The wife declares:

"Place me like a seal over your heart,
like a seal on your arm;
for love is as strong as death,
its jealousy unyielding as the grave.
It burns like blazing fire,
like a mighty flame.
Many waters cannot quench love;
rivers cannot sweep it away.
If one were to give
all the wealth of one's house for love,
it would be utterly scorned."
Song of Songs 8:6-7

"Like a seal over your heart." The best sexual love involves the heart. And not the momentary rush of emotions in the heart, but a deeper commitment of the heart—like a seal.

A seal in Bible times was used to "guarantee security or indicate ownership" (*Baker's Evangelical Dictionary of Biblical Theology*)—the kind of I'm-yours-you're-mine commitment that exists in a godly marriage. Indeed, the wife in Song of Songs says that very thing: *"My beloved is mine and I am his"* (2:16, also 6:3).

The way I think of it is the phrase "heart and soul." Which means completely, wholly, totally. In a sense, your sexual encounters should remind you of your wedding vows when you said to your mate, "This is it. I am *all in*."

Sometimes I fear we wives hold back on that emotional and spiritual connection with our husbands. Too many women feel that sex is merely a physical act—a pleasurable physiological experience or a release of body tension. But God intended it to mean so much more:

"Haven't you read," he replied, "that at the beginning the Creator 'made them male and female,' and said, 'For this reason a man will leave his father and mother and be united to his wife, and the two will become one flesh'? So they are no longer two, but one flesh. Therefore what God has joined together, let no one separate." Matthew 19:4-6

Look for ways to engage your heart and soul in lovemaking with your husband. Be tender, be active, be intimate. Express your love both verbally and physically in the bedroom. Remind yourself that sexuality is a gift for marriage from our Lord and Father—that it came from His own heart to bless ours.

Chapter 11
Dealing with a Low-desire Husband

Are you the higher-drive spouse? In some marriages, the wife is the one who desires sex more frequently and more intensely. That doesn't make you weird. It makes you like 15-25% of wives (statistics vary).

But sometimes, higher-drive wives feel like Vaquita porpoises (look it up; they're among the most endangered species). But forget the porpoise, and let's talk purpose. What's your mission as a higher-drive wife?

"All night long on my bed
I looked for the one my heart loves;
I looked for him but did not find him."
Song of Songs 3:1

143

Questions Higher-desire Wives Ask

Men are always the ones hot for sex, while women are lukewarm to cold much of the time. That's what society, and many churches now, tell us over and over. So it must be true, right?

No, it's not always true.

Some wives go day to day questioning what's wrong with them or their marital relationship because they desire a physically intimate relationship—but their hubby doesn't. It's the hush-hush secret we don't discuss, and these wives are silently suffering.

So what happens when a woman wants sex and her husband doesn't? Most women start to question. They wonder to themselves one or more of the following:

What's wrong with *me*? *If all husbands are panting and grabbing after their women 24/7 and my husband barely glances my direction when I don a sheer negligee, is there something about me that is distasteful? Am I unattractive? Why doesn't he find me physically pleasing?*

This likely isn't about your physical beauty. Your husband desired you enough to marry you. As long as you're reasonably keeping yourself up, your husband should find you attractive. If he doesn't, there is something amiss with his standards. There are things that many women can do to turn their hubbies' heads (flattering clothes, presentation, etc.), but a man who has almost no sex drive is probably not going to respond merely because you throw on a black lace teddy.

Is he having an affair? *If men think about sex every seven seconds and my hubby hasn't thought about it in three weeks, is he getting his fix elsewhere? Is he not pursuing me because he's already caught another woman?*

Some men are having affairs. But if you have no other clues in that direction, this is probably not the case. Moreover, married men in affairs may continue to have sex with their wives, so lack of interest isn't overwhelming evidence of infidelity. It's probably evidence of lack of interest, period.

Is he gay? *Is he simply not interested in sex with women generally? Is he desirous of another kind of relationship? Could he possibly be homosexual?*

There are no good statistics on how many spouses eventually "come out" as homosexual, but it isn't common. Once again, if you have no other hints that your husband could be gay, he most likely isn't. Lack of sex drive is not a good clue for sexual orientation.

Is our marriage over? *Does he not find me physically attractive because he is simply no longer in love with me?*

Does he not want a sexual relationship because he doesn't want any kind of relationship with me?

It's doubtful the marriage is over. If you have a good relationship otherwise, you can most likely improve the sexual area of your marital life as well. If you are not experiencing a good marital relationship overall, and your sex life is also poor, you should seek professional help. If your husband will not go with you, go alone and see if the counselor has suggestions for what you can do to positively impact you both.

Is something physically wrong with him? *Is there a medical or emotional problem getting in the way of his sex drive? Is he too embarrassed to admit it? Is he simply okay with not having sex?*

This is the most likely reason for your husband's lack of interest! A sufficient amount of testosterone is required for a man to experience a normal sex drive; if he is low on this hormone, his sex drive will decrease. Low thyroid hormone levels, depression, high blood sugar, and other factors can also affect your husband's libido. In addition, negative events of the past can impede a person's desire and enjoyment of sex with their partner. If a man was molested or inappropriately exposed to sexual material as a child, it can suppress his ability to engage in appropriate physical intimacy now. And increasingly, porn use has been implicated in the lowering of husbands' sex drives, by actually causing physiological changes in the brain's mode of arousal.

What can I do to improve our sex life? *If I bring up this subject, will I embarrass him? Will he be angry? Hurt? Even less attracted to me? Is there any fix available?*

Ultimately, you must bring up the topic if you want to see any improvement. If you are concerned that he will be embarrassed, angry, hurt, or whatever, schedule a therapy session with a Christian marriage counselor and address it in that safe environment. If you can address it with him alone, select a time away from the children, household interruptions, etc. and find a place with privacy and quiet.

Once you're able to sit and talk, do not complain about the lack of sex or unleash your theories about why he doesn't desire you; rather, explain that you are concerned about your physical relationship, that you desire greater physical intimacy, and that you want to address any and all issues that affect your lack of connection in that area. If there was a time when things were better, you can reference a "remember when…" and explain that you want to experience that closeness again.

Is this as good as it gets? *Am I relegated to a sexless marriage? If it never gets any better, how can I remain in this marriage? How can I be okay with that?*

I wish I could answer this one. A sexless marriage is *not* what God intended. Having said that, if my husband was physically injured tomorrow in a way that made it impossible for us to be physically intimate, would I stay? Absolutely! However, I understand that being unable to perform and unwilling to engage are two different things.

Spend time in prayer asking for God's help to work through the hurt and the loneliness you likely feel during this time. Sex is not the only reason to be married; there are many benefits to having a relationship with your husband.

Frankly, I don't know if men ask these questions of themselves when they are living in a sexless marriage. But women whose husbands have physically neglected them are probably going through a self-evaluation more extensive than the battery of tests given to a patient on psychiatric commitment. It's okay to ponder the problem, but not good to obsess and question every little thing about yourself or your marriage. Address the issue, seek help if needed, and pray for greater physical intimacy.

Internal Factors

If you are a wife with a higher sex drive than your husband, you're not alone. Plenty of woman deal with this issue. So how can you biblically and practically approach it with your husband?

Let's start with this gem: You cannot change your spouse.

You cannot make your spouse have sex with you. The transformation in your husband must come from him.

There are, however, internal and external factors that influence our decisions. For instance, I eat when I feel hungry (internal) and when someone puts a brownie in front of my face (external). *Don't judge.* I won't eat unless I make a decision to, but things happening in and around me impact my choices.

Internal factors are what's going on inside your husband. Internal factors may include:

- issues (past or present) with pornography that distort his perception of sexuality
- low testosterone
- depression
- a history of sexual abuse
- stress from job or other responsibilities
- guilt from prior promiscuity

- a lack of self-confidence

Just as you can't control your husband's hunger, you can't control factors impacting his low sexual drive. Yet you can help him identify what's happening. Unfortunately, we often choose the worst ways to get him to recognize the problem:

- nagging
- pleading
- demanding
- shoving information and research in his face
- sharing the story of your cousin or your friend's husband
- over-the-top crying
- quoting scripture at him
- threatening
- giving ultimatums
- saying, "If you loved me, you'd…"

These tactics make conversation unpleasant and tense, and many husbands will run from that faster than the Roadrunner from Wile E. Coyote.

Yes, 1 Corinthians 7:4-5a says: *"The wife's body does not belong to her alone but also to her husband. In the same way, the husband's body does not belong to him alone but also to his wife. Do not deprive each other except by mutual consent and for a time, so that you may devote yourselves to prayer."* That verse indicates that it's a sin to deprive one another; the Bible commands us not to. How can we point out that sin?

Yet consider Matthew 7:12: *"So in everything, do to others what you would have them do to you..."* If a husband is struggling with depression, a pornography addiction, past abuse, or whatever, he doesn't want to be slammed on the head with what else is wrong with him. But he does need to deal with the issues. Ask yourself how you can create a safe environment for the two of you to openly discuss marital intimacy.

Find a good place and time to talk. The worst place is in the bedroom and the worst time is after you've offered sex and he's declined. Choose a time when you are not sexually charged or feeling particularly hurt. You may even need to get away from the house, although make sure you're in a private setting. Keep your clothes on. Men often talk more easily shoulder-to-shoulder than face-to-face, so try a fishing trip, golfing, a nature hike, touring a sculpture garden— whatever suits your fancy and his.

Don't make statements. Ask questions.

- How do you think our marriage is going overall?
- Growing up, who were your role models for marriage? How do you think they influenced you?
- What do you wish you had done differently before marriage regarding sexuality? What are you glad you did right?

- Before we married, what did you think married sex life would be like?
  - What would you like our sex life to be like?
  - How frequently would you like to make love?
  - What turns you on? What turns you off?
  - How can I be a better lover to you?

Now don't grill the poor guy. This isn't the Spanish Inquisition where you expect him to recant his heresy and adopt your doctrine on the spot. Choose a question or two at a time and let the conversation unfold. It may take several outings and weeks or even months to get to the heart of the problems. But you aren't simply gathering information. You're demonstrating by your attitude and approach that you're a trustworthy confidante regarding this topic and want the best for both of you.

Adopt a "we" attitude. Whatever his issue is, treat it as a *we* problem. Even if he brought some problem into the marriage, it is yours to tackle *together*. You're married—one flesh. Indeed, he could return that favor if someday you struggle with hormonal issues or depression that affects your own libido. Assure him that whatever the issue is, you aren't there to wave it around in front of him. You want to be the helper that God described in Genesis 2:18.

Express your desire for intimacy, not just frequency. No one likes to be used. Which is one of the reasons why a lower-drive spouse can react like prodded cobra when the higher-drive spouse says they want more sex. They may not feel loved so much as used to meet a physical need.

Of course, you know and I know that's not the reality. If you only wanted to release sexual tension, you could get that done without engaging your husband. Sex, however, is a physical expression of closeness and also fosters closeness between you. Focus your discussion on how you desire to engage with your husband in intimacy because you desire that closeness.

Ask for a win-win. Ask your husband to help you find a win-win solution that's not merely a compromise but meets both parties' needs and desires. You may require a mediator to find that win-win. Perhaps he'll agree to meet a few times with a counselor or your pastor and brainstorm ways for both of you to get what you want out of your intimacy.

Pray. Cover every step with prayer. And don't make it, "Dear God, please change my husband from being a selfish, ignorant jerk to a sweet, passionate lover."

Pray for your husband to have the delight of sex with you. Pray for you to delight in him. Pray for you to reach accord. Pray the scripture itself when words fail you, and when they don't. For instance, pray Proverbs 5:18-19. Here's my translation: "Dear God, I pray that my husband's fountain will be blessed, that he will find reasons to rejoice in me and our marriage. I pray that he will see me as loving and graceful and that my breasts will always satisfy him. I pray that he will become intoxicated by my love." Can I get an "Amen" for that?

Remember that you can't change your husband. The person you can control is *you*! Decide to take that deep breath, commit to being the best wife you can be, and do what you can to create a more intimate marriage.

External Factors

About one-fourth of the time, the wife is the higher-desire spouse. This reality is the secret that never gets discussed because:

(1) What husband wants to admit he isn't the stereotypical, sex-craving man?

(2) Wives who express their desire for more sex are often shut down by other wives with statements like, "I wish my husband would lay off" or even "You're lucky."

(3) We tend to discuss all topics from the point of view of the "typical." Don't believe me? Read a parenting book. If only my kid was the "average," my child would have slept through the night within weeks, stayed in time-out after three tries, and potty-trained at age two. Yeah, that didn't happen. Likewise, no person or marriage is "average" or "normal" in every way, and some marriages have a higher-desire wife.

In the last chapter, I covered Internal Factors that might affect a husband's lack of interest in sex and gave some tips for bringing up the subject without starting a wildfire in your home.

A few wives report that the husband won't listen, no matter what. If that's your situation, here's my advice: Stop talking about it. "Wait," you say, "how are we going to solve the problem if we can't even address it?" I'm not saying to stop addressing it, I'm saying to stop addressing it with *words*. If the subject is so volatile in your house, you both need time to defuse. Lay off for a while, maybe three to six months. In the meantime, communicate—but not with words.

For both those marriages where the husband will listen and those where the husband won't, external factors might increase your mate's interest in sex. As I stated before, I eat when I'm hungry (internal) and when someone places a brownie in front of me (external). While talking with your husband can help reveal and address internal factors, you can also influence him externally. Let's take a look at this approach.

Your words and actions can be external factors (like brownies) that make him more likely to want to have sex (eat). You want to be the kind of wife that would draw a husband closer. You want to *be the brownie*.

Note that I say *be* a particular kind of person, not just look sexy, throw yourself at your husband, etc. Some suggest the way to get an uninterested husband's sexual attention is to don a lace teddy and stilettos, call him "Big Boy," and offer to live out some sexual fantasy.

While I'm not opposed to such things, they're the toppings, not the cake. You might get a guy to have sex with you by looking like a *Cosmo* cover, but that's not marital intimacy. Ultimately, you want a sex life with substance and intimacy, so you have to invest in the relationship cake before you add a little icing.

Moreover, you can end up feeling worse if you decorate your bedroom like a love den, put on candles and music, show up in your sexiest get-up, and he ignores or outright refuses you. You don't want to end that night with him snoring and you dripping tears into your pillow as you wonder what's wrong with you.

Let me help you out with that issue too: There's almost certainly nothing wrong with you. Some couples with amazing sex lives would never get a call from a modeling agency or were poster people for the geek club in high school. It's a fallacy to think that rock stars and Victoria's Secret models are the ones with high sex drives and satisfaction. Maybe, maybe not. Most wives don't need to look like Jessica Rabbit to get their hubbies hopping. The problem most likely lies within your husband.

But getting back to the subject at hand, how can you *be the brownie?*

Invest in the friendship. Sheila Gregoire has pointed this out well in her book, *The Good Girl's Guide to Great Sex.* You want to be the kind of wife your husband wants to be around generally and then you can move toward being together sexually. When the relationship is stressful, it's harder for most people to engage willingly and become vulnerable in the bedroom.

Do everything in your power (knowing that it doesn't all rest with you) to be an appealing person. Are you a nagging person? Do you disrespect him with your words or your body language? Is your home always a place of tension or mayhem? What negative issues might you need to address?

Have you forgotten how to play and laugh with one another? Do you make time for a date night—even if it's hot cocoa and conversation on the couch after the kids have gone to bed? Do you ask about his job, his interests, his friendships, and then listen and support his answers? Do you find activities that you both enjoy doing together?

Your husband may be more willing to discuss the issues and/or engage with you physically if he feels accepted and valued emotionally in the relationship. Make sure you haven't neglected this area. You want him to be your friend, right? Be his friend too.

Focus on affection. While friendship is an important aspect of marriage, sexless marriages often look like roommate arrangements with friends. I don't know about you, but I have friends who would make easier roommates than my husband. Some of my girlfriends can cook like a Food Network show host, would aim at my toilet more successfully, could watch chick flicks with me, etc., and I'd never have to clean facial hair out of the sink again. I didn't get married simply for a roommate. I want the other goodies too.

But even if you aren't getting the main event, you can get more than you would from a roomie. I don't snuggle with my BFF, but I do with my husband. Physical affection is a precursor to more intimate physical affection. Hold hands, kiss, hug, stroke him lovingly, etc. All without expectation of it leading to the bedroom.

The paradox is that ongoing physical affection without the expectation of sexual reward more often leads to sexual reward. Moreover, an embrace lasting longer than 20 seconds can cause a release of oxytocin—the body's bonding chemical which is also released by men at sexual climax. So affection may awaken the physical arousal side of your husband, and it introduces loving touch in a low-pressure context.

Engage in skin-to-skin contact. Beyond simple physical affection, try to engage in skin-to-skin contact. There is something about having your skin brush up against your husband's that can tap into inner arousal. Go to bed wearing as little as possible without being obvious that you want sex. For instance, keep the lace teddy in the drawer, but wear a cotton cami and undies to bed. Play footsie under the table at breakfast. Offer to put lotion or oil on his tired muscles or give him a massage. Ask for lotion or a massage yourself. Whatever gets you touching each other may help to reawaken his natural desire for physical intimacy.

Change your timing. Some people struggle with feeling stressed or tired by nightfall and having enough energy for lovemaking. You might try initiating sex in the morning since a man's testosterone levels are highest at that time of day, and men typically awaken with a "maintenance erection." I know a couple who has sex like clockwork every Saturday morning; that happens to be the best time for them to engage. My hubby and I have found that an afternoon or early evening are often better for us. If nighttime has been your usual window for sex, see if you have better results at a different time of day.

Once again, you can do all the "right things" and still have an uninterested husband. Your sex life doesn't all depend upon you; your husband must make the decision to engage. But be assured that I hear from married couples who had poor sex lives for years, experienced a turn-around, and are now livin' it up in the bedroom. Those couples are glad they didn't give up.

Also, if you're in a sexless marriage, you may reach the point of needing to invite intervention from a godly mentor. Your husband does indeed have a duty to you and to the marriage (1 Corinthians 7:3-5). You are supposed to be "one flesh" —emotionally and physically.

Are there guarantees? No. Is there hope? Absolutely. God desires you both to have a healthy, fulfilling intimacy, and He can redeem any situation.

Chapter 12
Addressing Physical Pain

I wish I could say that God is completely opposed to any and all pain. But when you read the story of God's people, you find that He's not against letting us suffer through pain for His higher purposes. Honestly, this life is going to have some pain, but God will help us bear it.

Sexual pain is not in that category. When it comes to sexual intimacy, God is definitely in favor of health and pleasure. There isn't some higher purpose in physically hurting when you don't need to. Let life hand you lemons when it must, but sex with your husband should be more like chocolate. Right?

> **"[Jesus] had compassion on them
> and healed their sick."
> Matthew 14:14b**

What to Do When Sex Is Painful

Here I am, along with other Christian bloggers, encouraging women to have great intimate encounters with their husbands, and some women continue to resist. Because for some of you, when it comes down to it, intercourse is like inserting a serrated knife into your ear—or worse. Sex flat out hurts.

This is absolutely not an area in which "No Pain, No Gain" applies. Sex is not supposed to be physically painful. If it is, do not grit your teeth and bear it. Treat it like any other instance of pain in your body. If you had ongoing migraines, you'd try to find out why and treat them. If you had excruciating back pain, you'd see your doctor, a chiropractor, or a massage therapist. If you had sharp pangs every time you walked, you wouldn't stop walking altogether or decide that painful walking was your personal normal; you'd say to yourself, "Hey, what's up? Walking isn't supposed to hurt!"

Remember that God designed sex in marriage to provide intimacy and pleasure. That is what He desires for you. So what can you do to address pain during intercourse?

Examination. Visit your doctor and see if there's a physical reason for your pain. Cervical structure, low estrogen, and other factors can negatively impact your comfort during intercourse. Physical causes of sexual pain can be addressed.

After childbirth, intercourse with my husband felt like having a scythe inserted vaginally. At my third visit to the gynecologist, the physician's assistant realized that my estrogen was especially low. She prescribed a cream, and *voilà!* pain alleviated. It was a relief to me and my husband that I could engage in intimate encounters without wincing, crying buckets, and begging (internally) for him to finish. Thank goodness we discovered the physical cause and treated it.

Preparation. If physical factors are not to blame, it could be that the husband is entering his wife too soon. A woman needs adequate lubrication and swelling to receive a penis without discomfort. The inner vaginal lips (or labia minora) must swell to perhaps three times their regular size, as arousal causes blood flow to this area. If the woman is not moist enough or swollen enough, her body requires more preparation. Preparation = foreplay.

Women take longer to heat up. Make sure you allow time to become sufficiently aroused. If necessary, designate a specified time for foreplay. Tell hubby that you need 15 minutes of love play before entry. Or a certain number of romantic songs playing in the background can be your timer. Make sure that you are ready for your husband's penis. If you are, it will likely feel quite good when he enters.

Lubrication. It can be difficult, at times, to produce enough lubrication on your own. Perhaps it's a time of the month when hormones are less cooperative, or the couple doesn't have sufficient time in the schedule for long foreplay, or aging is playing its part in slowing down the juices. Whatever the reason, purchase a lubricant and keep it near your bed. Try different brands to find the one you like best. You can apply the lubricant yourself or ask your hubby to do so (a request he'd likely oblige).

Moisture in the vaginal area assists with stimulation and pleasure. Your husband's fondling may not feel good without that wetness. If you aren't producing it on your own, don't worry about it. Just apply lubrication.

Experimentation. Find out what feels good to you. A lot of women who claim they don't like sex have merely accepted the method used by their husband, and what he does doesn't feel good. Try different ways of touching one another, different positions, or different times for entry or ways of thrusting. This isn't a perfect-on-the-first-try activity. Explore one another's bodies and learn what's enjoyable.

Prior to childbirth, I had a tilted uterus, and sex often felt more comfortable when my husband entered my vagina from behind. A little experimentation led us to discover a position that kept me from experiencing pain and intensified my pleasure. Of course, my enjoyment made the encounter more enjoyable for my husband as well. Free yourself to find out what brings you pleasure and what brings pain, so you can pursue the former and avoid the latter.

Communication. Talk to your husband about what feels good and what doesn't. If you begin to feel discomfort or pain, let him know. He isn't a mind reader. Most men are not so absorbed by their own desire for climax that they don't care about injuring you. Loving husbands want their wives to gain pleasure from having sex with them. So communicate.

This may mean piping up verbally during the event to say, "Ooh, that doesn't feel good. How about this?" Or it may mean guiding his hand or his penis where you want it. It can also entail sitting down outside the bedroom and having a heart-to-heart conversation about the pain you experience and your desire to experience pleasure instead. Your husband will probably be happy to discuss options for accomplishing that goal.

Habituation. Sex needs to happen with some regularity for pain or soreness to be avoided. If I try to run five miles, my legs are going to scream bloody murder at me, and I will awaken the next morning barely able to move. If I don't run again until three months later, it will still hurt like the dickens. But if I run today, tomorrow, the next day, and so on, I will be able to run five miles before I know it with a runner's high instead of a weakling's cramping.

Some women experience unnecessary pain because they do not engage in sex often enough for their muscles to adapt. Vaginas stretch a little with use. The vagina will still be tight enough to cause pleasure for the man, but it needs to remain elastic enough to respond. If sex hurts and you don't have sex again for three months, it will likely hurt just as much the next time. Making sex a habit gets your body used to the physical activity, increasing the likelihood that you will enjoy the experience.

Remember that sex isn't supposed to hurt. See if one of these reasons is causing the problem and address it immediately. Bring your husband in on the deal and enlist his help.

Chapter 13
Defining "Christian Sex"

The clearest way of expressing my mission in writing a Christian sex blog is: "Christians need to reclaim sexuality."

Satan and the world have tried to make it theirs—although a twisted version of what God created. It's not theirs. It belongs to God and to His people. To married Christians. At least the best sex does...the sex that pleases one another, expresses covenant love, and grows intimacy.

But what is "Christian sex"? What does our spiritual faith have to do with physical pleasure?

Quite a lot actually.

"As a bridegroom rejoices over his bride,
so will your God rejoice over you."
Isaiah 62:5

Godly Sex Is Complex

In one sense, sex is simple. Intercourse requires the couple to insert Tab A into Slot B, remove, and repeat.

But a healthy sexual relationship requires much, much more. The barriers to a healthy relationship primarily exist in one of three areas.

Unhealthy attitude. This is where healthy sex *must* begin. You can hear oodles and oodles of fabulous fixes and techniques, but if one spouse approaches the other and marital intimacy with an unhealthy attitude, such ideas won't bring about a fulfilling relationship.

The biggest barrier to a good attitude is self. It can be the self-pleasuring of a mate who spends hours looking at online pornography, the self-focus of being too tired or too body conscious to make love, or the self-preservation instinct of someone who was molested in their childhood years. Yes, this is a wide range of issues, but a healthy sexual relationship must begin with prioritizing relational intimacy above one's self. Let me be clear: These reasons for lack of sexual intimacy are not all selfishness, but they are about self. For some, putting the marriage first means a simple attitude adjustment; for others it requires deep self-examination or therapy to heal from a painful history.

Perhaps the toughest situations I hear about are those in which one spouse has worked hard to have a great attitude toward sexual intimacy in marriage and the other spouse is a selfish blockhead. No amount of sex education will make make the selfish person a terrific lover because godly sexuality isn't ultimately about arousal or orgasm; it's about expressing and fostering mutual intimacy through deep physical contact.

Specific sexual problems. Some people want a better sex life, but they have specific issues that need to be addressed. Perhaps a spouse has low desire, difficulty with arousal, a pornography addiction, physical exhaustion, interrupting kids, a lack of knowledge about the human body, etc. There's a myriad of barriers to a fulfilling sex life that have to do with addressing something specific in the person or the relationship.

At times, I have dealt with such issues, such as painful sex or past mistreatment. Many problems can be tackled with awareness and effort. Yet, some require the intervention of a counselor or physician. The first step here is being able to identify what problems you have in your specific relationship. Your marriage is not exactly like anyone else's. However, for just about every specific problem, there is a fix. It may be a quick tweak or a long-term program to get things right, but there are couples everywhere who have overcome all kinds of difficulties to become sexually intimate and satisfied in their marriage.

Don't give up on working toward something better. For instance, if your physician has dismissed your inability to become aroused, find another physician. Look for answers. Find help. Making your sex life a priority means tackling the barriers to marital intimacy.

Failure to nurture. Having planted the seed of a good attitude toward marital sexuality and then seeing sprouts come up as you deal with specific problems, married couples cannot simply relax and expect to reap a never-ending harvest of sexual satisfaction. Intimacy must be nurtured.

Couples must make time to engage in sexuality; if they don't, then work, household tasks, children, church activities, friends, recreation, and more will crowd it out. You must stay in communication with each other about what you want from your sex life— which may change. What felt great five years ago to your mate may not be the same now. Moreover, physical changes in your body (pregnancy, age, etc.) may present challenges you need to deal with.

We must remind ourselves of the importance of sexuality and make efforts to deal with issues that crop up over time. We need to keep our attitude toward our husband and our marital intimacy where it should be.

Information and encouragement, as well as knowing and applying the Word of God to your sex life, can help substantially. If you wistfully recall your first year of marriage being a veritable sex feast and now simply sit around and wonder what happened to the delicious goodies, then you'll never achieve the long-term marital intimacy God desires for you. Nurture your relationship. And that nurturing will look different in different seasons.

Godly sex is complex. Because there are so many ways in which Satan attacks us in our sexual lives — with poor attitudes, annoying and serious problems, and complacency.

Since I (and no other author, speaker, therapist, etc.) can see directly into your sex life, it's up to you as a married couple to figure out where the barriers are and how you want to move past them. I deliver information, support, a little humor, and prayers that husbands and wives will work on their intimacy and discover God's beautiful gift of sexuality in marriage.

Those of you who continue to struggle pierce my heart and make me fall to my knees. I know that our Heavenly Father wants the best for His beloved children, and that includes you. It is my sincere hope that this book and my blog help to shine light on the blessings our Lord has for us.

The Gospel in the Bedroom

We don't usually see the words "gospel" and "bedroom" in the same sentence.

Yet, the Gospel is the central point of Christianity. Jesus Christ, God's only Son, entered the world in human form; lived and preached among us; sacrificed Himself as the ultimate blood offering for our sins; and conquered death through His resurrection so that we can live with our Lord eternally. That is definitely good news, or gospel, to the whole world.

The Gospel calls us to higher principles, purposeful lives, and servant hearts. Often, we don't allow it to permeate every area of our lives. The Gospel should impact what you choose to do with your time and money, which thoughts you dwell on and which ones you resist, how you treat your friends and the restaurant drive-through employee, and—believe it or not—how you approach the marital bedroom.

The Gospel matters a great deal in every aspect of life, including the intimacy you experience with your husband. Here are just a few aspects of the Gospel that affect your married sex life:

Because of Christ, you can trust that God can redeem your brokenness.

"In him we have redemption through his blood, the forgiveness of sins, in accordance with the riches of God's grace that he lavished on us with all wisdom and understanding." Ephesians 1:7

If you have sexual baggage from your past—an addiction to pornography, promiscuity before your marriage, an affair that wrecked the trust in your bedroom, or whatever other sin you can think of—Jesus Christ died for that sin. He brings forgiveness and healing when you confess and repent.

Because of Christ, you can forgive your husband and give grace.

"Bear with each other and forgive whatever grievances you may have against one another. Forgive as the Lord forgave you." Colossians 3:13

Has your husband mistreated you sexually at some time? Sought his own pleasure and ignored yours? Belittled your sexual needs? Demanded sexual satisfaction or refrained from giving himself fully? Quite honestly, most of us can think of a time when our husband was selfish regarding sexuality. But regardless of what has happened in the past, you can be generous, give grace, start over.

Give your hubby the benefit of the doubt. For instance, maybe he awakened you to have sex last night at 3:00 a.m. not because he doesn't care how exhausted you were after taking care of a sick child yesterday or working on a job project with a looming deadline; maybe he was restless and started thinking about how beautiful you are to him. We can't know our husband's exact motives, so lean toward the most positive possibility. And forgive past sins, as you have been forgiven.

Because of Christ, you can have hope for your future.

"I pray also that the eyes of your heart may be enlightened in order that you may know the hope to which he has called you, the riches of his glorious inheritance in the saints, and his incomparably great power for us who believe. That power is like the working of his mighty strength, which he exerted in Christ when he raised him from the dead and seated him at his right hand in the heavenly realms." Ephesians 1:18-20

Think about that. The same power that God used to resurrect His Son is working in your life. You have hope for better things—in the life after this one, and in this life as well. We know that Jesus wants our lives and marriages to be full (John 10:10), loving (Ephesians 5:2), and fulfilling (1 Corinthians 7:3). When we know that God desires for us to have intimacy in our marriage and then shares His power with us, we have hope! Maybe your marriage and sex life isn't everything it should be. Continue in prayer. Continue in faith. Continue in hope.

Because of Christ, your body has intrinsic value.

"Do you not know that your body is a temple of the Holy Spirit, who is in you, whom you have received from God? You are not your own; you were bought at a price. Therefore honor God with your body." 1 Corinthians 6:19-20

Your body is valuable and has the capacity to honor God. The verse prior says to "flee from sexual immorality," and then gives the above reason. But if you are fleeing from sexual immorality, what should you run to? Well, to sexual morality, of course! Welcome to God's plan. You honor God with your body when you follow His plan for it in marriage; when you delight in the mate your Father has given you; when you seal your commitment and intimacy with physical bonding.

Because of Christ, you know what true love is.

"A new command I give you: Love one another. As I have loved you, so you must love one another." John 13:34

I teared up while looking for passages for this one. There are *so many* to choose from. We know what true love looks like because Jesus modeled it for us. He was patient with disciples, gentle with sinners, humble before God, and serving and sacrificial above all. Imagine taking the perfect love of Jesus into the bedroom and being patient, gentle, serving, and sacrificial. Imagine *both* of you approaching physical intimacy that way. Now tell me how fabulous that would be for your sex life.

Because of Christ, you know that your intimacy mirrors and symbolizes what the Church has with Jesus, her Bridegroom.

"'For this reason a man will leave his father and mother and be united to his wife, and the two will become one flesh.' This is a profound mystery—but I am talking about Christ and the church." Ephesians 5:31-32

Isn't it amazing that the verse chosen to reflect Christ and the church ends with "the two will become one flesh"? The unity of a husband and wife is like Christ's unity with His people. I desire one day to have with my Lord the intimacy that mirrors the intense closeness I experience with my husband in the midst of sex. How I long for it! And when I experience such pleasure and bonding with my husband, I know that it is a mere taste of what God has waiting for us in Heaven.

If the Gospel is true, the implications move into every aspect of our life. Our marriages are affected by God's steadfast, redeeming love. Our physical intimacy with our mate is affected by His example and sacrifice.

We Christians need not approach the bedroom as the world does. Sex isn't merely physical or all about oneself. The apex of intimacy is not multiple orgasms or more and more kinky sexual acts. The goal isn't to have sex *when* we want, *with whom* we want, *however* we want, *wherever* we want without regard to others. We have the ultimate instead: a Gospel-driven life that shows a better way in every area—including the marital bedroom. And guess what? With God's perfect design, we can end up having the most amazing sex!

I pray for each married couple to experience the Gospel in their bedroom—to know the overwhelming love of Christ and to share it with their spouse.

"And I pray that you, being rooted and established in love, may have power, together with all the saints, to grasp how wide and long and high and deep is the love of Christ, and to know this love that surpasses knowledge—that you may be filled to the measure of all the fullness of God." Ephesians 3:17-19

Chapter 14
Bonus: Calling Us to Ministry

There is a growing awareness that individual Christians and church communities need to speak up, not merely against ungodly sexuality but also in favor of godly sexuality.

Speaking up isn't always easy. Some believe we shouldn't talk about it because the act itself is between two exclusive, committed persons. But God doesn't shy away from the subject of sex. It's all through Scripture. We can have a public conversation about sex without compromising our ultimate privacy.

So let's join Peter and John in their prayer:

"Enable your servants to speak your word with great boldness."
Acts 4:29b

Step Up, Church, and Talk about Sex

How should Christians and the Church in general address the subject of sexuality?

Take a look at the letters of Paul in the New Testament. He boldly addresses whatever issue plagues the church and refocuses people on God's desire for their lives.

Wrongful thinking and behaviors regarding sex permeate our culture. From the sexually abused child to the promiscuous teen to the porn-addicted husband to the withholding wife to the married couple who struggles to connect physically, we are off target a lot. Jesus never turned a blind eye to sin and pain in His midst. It is our God-given duty to speak into others' pain and confusion, to speak for God where He has spoken, and to pass on God's desire for their lives, even in the area of sexuality.

What should this boldness look like? Ideally, churches should have a cradle-to-grave approach. Here are my suggestions for how churches can minister to people in various stages:

CHILDREN/TEENS

Provide parenting classes to help families address the subject. Plenty of parents want to equip their children with a godly view of sexuality, but they simply don't know how to talk to their kids about it.

Empower youth ministry to address biblical sexuality with tweens and teens. All too often, parents resist having the subject brought up in church. Guess what? It's being brought up everywhere else your kid is. Isn't it better for our children to get information from a biblically-driven youth pastor rather than rely on his/her school friend or a TV show?

Host fun, well-supervised teen events. Churches can help teens by hosting events that provide opportunities to mingle and have fun without the sexual temptation that often exists in secular venues. It needs to be something that will attract teens, but also keep them out of pressurized situations. For instance, when I was a teen, a couple of churches hosted teen dances; the likelihood of anything inappropriate happening with my date at his Mormon church's family dance was practically nil. Here's another out-of-the-box idea: What if a church rented a bunch of luxury cars and had volunteer members drive teenagers and their dates to and from local proms?

SINGLES

Provide pre-engagement and premarital classes and counseling. There are some excellent studies for dating couples. Ask most married couples if they wish they had prepared more, and they'll say yes—including in the area of sexual intimacy.

Help singles find a mate. I don't believe everyone must get married or that being single is a lesser status. However, 1 Corinthians 7:9 says, *"It is better to marry than to burn with passion."* And, although marriage rates are declining in the U.S., the vast majority of people still want to be married at some point. Hey, the best thing the church ever did for my sex life was to introduce me to my husband. But too many single Christians have few options. What can churches do? They can offer area-wide singles events. I'm not suggesting some Christian version of The Bachelor or The Dating Game. Such events shouldn't be meat markets, but rather worship, fellowship, or Bible studies which allow singles to gather and get to know one another. Love can take it from there.

MARRIEDS

Make marriage classes, retreats, and seminars routine. In addition to in-depth scriptural and theological studies, churches should teach on the practical application of God's Word. Look for biblically-based marriage studies or find couples with knowledge to share.

Stop skipping the sex part! This is part B of the above suggestion. I was once told by another marriage blogger that churches often skip the sex lesson in a marriage series—perhaps because the topic is considered too sensitive. That tidbit of information had me V8-headsmacking the rest of the day. God wants married couples to have growing marriages and great sex! Let's support healthy marriages by helping couples do exactly that.

Financially support marriage ministries. Many quality marriage resources can only continue through outside financial support, and churches can make that a goal of their budget.

Provide babysitting services to married couples with children. One of the hardest periods for marital intimacy is when the kids are young. A group of church members (e.g., youth, "Golden Agers," singles) could provide babysitting as a ministry. Or a church could establish a babysitting co-op in which couples keep each others' kids at times and then get their own date nights.

MISCELLANEOUS

Take a sex survey of your church and present your findings. Oftentimes, we don't know that church members are struggling with sexuality. Who's going to stand up on Sunday morning and say, "Could you address biblical sexuality because I ain't gettin' any at home?" We can awaken the attention of church leaders and members by asking for anonymous input about where they are thriving and where they need help.

Be specific. Churches often address sexuality at too high a level. For singles, we hear, "God wants you to stay pure." Yes, He does. But be specific about how a sexually-ramped-up 17-year-old boy can stay cool when a hot girl throws herself at him. Or how a 23-year-old single woman can wait another seven years to let her libido see daylight? For the marrieds, it isn't enough to say, "God wants you to have a good sex life." How does a husband figure out how to pleasure his wife to climax? How can a women deal with her lagging interest in sex? How can a couple move beyond negative sexual histories? Be specific.

Bring in special speakers. Christian colleges and universities often have marriage and family therapy or Christian ministry departments with qualified experts. There are also writers, bloggers, counselors, and speakers who address this subject.

Offer couples counseling. Couples counseling should be available to dating teens, couples in serious relationships, engaged couples, and married couples. The singles may need a session or two to learn strategies for stopping sexual activity before it starts, while a married couple may need to address a lack of intimacy or physical barriers to satisfying sex. If the church does not have the wherewithal to offer such counseling, it can subsidize another church's counseling center or a Christian-based counseling practice.

Plug into ministries that help those who need special care. Has a child been sexually abused? Is a husband dealing with a porn addiction? Is a couple dealing with adultery? Such issues go beyond typical couples counseling. Find ministries that address specific issues.

Look for experts in your midst. That physician who attends your church? The labor and delivery nurse? The psychologist or counselor? The recovering sex addict? The woman who was sexually abused as a child and found healing? The couple that lived through an affair and have a thriving marriage? They have something to offer. Ask how they are willing to help support healthy and godly sex lives for church members.

Maintain a quality library with helpful resources on biblical sexuality. There are many Christian-based books and video and audio series available, but cost can be prohibitive for families. Churches could purchase resources, then let families know what's available.

No one church can offer all of this, so we must rely on each other in the larger church body. But each church can address godly sexuality throughout the seasons of life by offering biblical knowledge, specific information, relationship support, and prayer for the purity and intimacy of their members.

What does your church do to boldly address biblical sexuality? What can you do?

Acknowledgements

In December 2010, I answered the Holy Spirit's nudging and started a blog about marriage and sexuality—*Hot, Holy & Humorous.* I hoped that posting once a week and getting maybe a hundred visitors would be a success and would also, quite frankly, get God off my back. I had long felt the need to speak up in favor of God's design for sexuality in marriage, but I was happy to do so only as opportunities presented. Pursuing that as a ministry wasn't on my to-do list.

God had other plans.

Almost three years into blogging, I now glance at the number of hits on my blog and fall off my office chair. (Don't worry: I have carpeting.) I knew there was a need for Christian wives to know more about sex and how it impacts marriage, but I had no idea God was going to use *little ol' me* to reach people across the United States and the world; to provide information, encouragement, and entertainment about sex in marriage; to speak into the lives of so many couples to help them experience the blessings that God has for married couples if they pursue His design.

Thus, I owe many thanks to...

My Lord and Savior. *"To whom shall I go? You have the words of eternal life.*[6]*"* You alone know what disaster my life would have been without You. I am amazed that You would save me from my premarital promiscuous ways and their negative consequences and then utterly blown away that You would bless me with such intimacy and pleasure in my enduring marriage.

My illustrator. Matt Baxter did such an excellent job. Thanks, Matt, for simple, beautiful drawings that represented the topics so well, yet remained tasteful, and for the book cover illustration which I call my "sex savvy woman." I thank God for your talent and your willingness to use it.

My editor. Julie, thanks for clearing up my oopses and my confusing language where needed. It's marvelous to have someone I can wholly trust with my words. And yes, I still owe you a glass of Cabernet.

My readers and followers. Wow! I could write another book with the insight and encouragement my readers have provided. You keep me on my toes by

---

[6] John 6:68.

asking great questions and sharing your own stories of sorrow and redemption.

My fellow bloggers. If I listed them all, I'd need several pages. But a few deserve a spotlight. Sheila Wray Gregoire was quick to start promoting my posts and has been a role model in the way she speaks boldly for God. Julie Sibert of *Intimacy in Marriage* gave me my first guest post opportunity and then became one of my best friends—sharing a love for baseball, good wine, black licorice, and hot and holy sex. Paul and Lori Byerly of *Generous Husband, Generous Wife,* and *The Marriage Bed* are two of the most incredible people you could know in the marriage ministry world. And the graceful Debi Walter of *The Romantic Vineyard* inspired the chapter on The Gospel in the Bedroom. The Christian Marriage Bloggers Association also has many members who have informed and encouraged me in this ministry. Thanks to all of you!

My best friend, "C." I have the best friends, and you in particular have discussed God and sexuality with me for years, giving me the opportunity to flesh out what godly sexuality really looks like. You also listened to many of my drafted posts and laughed in all the right places. I'm so excited to spend this life and the next hanging out with you, C.

My family. Thank you for not freaking out when I told you I'd been called a "sexpert" and for your ongoing support.

My husband, whom my readers know as "Spock." You've lived through the good, the bad, and the "you rock my world!" years with me. I love you more now than ever. (Psst, race you to the bedroom!)

About the Author

J writes at *Hot, Holy & Humorous,* where she uses a biblical perspective and a blunt sense of humor to foster Christian sexuality in marriage.

When she isn't writing about godly sex or doing "research" with her husband, J writes teen fiction; hugs, disciplines, or cracks jokes with her kids (whichever is needed in the moment); and daydreams about having a personal chef and an on-call massage therapist.

Check out J's blog at www.hotholyhumorous.com or follow her on Twitter at @hotholyhumorous, Facebook at HotHolyHumorous, or Pinterest at hotholyhumorous.

14496219R00109

Made in the USA
San Bernardino, CA
31 August 2014